Trout A

And Other Uncomfortable Truths

Walt Fulps

Contents

Dedication

This is the easiest section of this book to write. My wife Linda is the only person who really understands the time and effort that has gone into this book, the starts and stops, the doubts and resolve, and the frustrations. And she never had a negative word to say… other than "you still aren't done with that thing?"

The smartest thing I've ever done was marry you.

PROLOGUE

Psych 101 and Stupid Ducks

Humans throughout history have made up stories and rules to explain the things around them that they do not understand and we've done the same thing to explain trout. They're confusing and infuriating and moody and yet beautiful and alluring — kind of romantic, right? We must have them and yet they will often not be had, in spite of our intelligence and best efforts. I'm old enough that my instinct is to refer to those stories as "old wives tales," but my wife disapproves so we'll call them "fish stories" instead.

Many American trout fishermen first learned to fish by chasing warm water species, eventually converting to cold water fish enthusiasts. There's a reason grandpa started you out this way, using a worm and a bobber to catch a bluegill or casting shad sides in search of a channel cat. Warm water fish make more sense to most of us. They act the way a fish "should" act.

Cold water fish act differently so there must be a logical reason, right? Right! When the logic escapes us, however, we tend to make up our own explanations. We develop myths and believe me when I say trout knowledge is loaded with superstition. Throughout this book, we'll address a good number of them, including the most prominent of them all.

Fish story: Trout are smart.

Trout are not much smarter than the insects they eat. I was 11 years old when this first occurred to me. One bright spring day after school, I decided to skip riding the bus and walked home instead. This allowed me the opportunity to stop by Roubidoux Creek, the stream that runs through downtown Waynesville, Missouri ... the waters where I first learned to catch trout. I spent every moment I could there, gazing into the waters looking for turtles, muskrats, and of course fish.

This particular day, I found a beat up old "fur bug" on the bank, which is what we called trout flies consisting of nothing but a bit of fuzzy yarn wrapped around a hook. Feeling I'd discovered a bit of treasure, I picked it up. A bit further upstream, I noticed a small rainbow trout spooking out of his spot a few feet from the bank. I studied the water in an attempt to find where he'd run off to and was quite surprised to see him return to his spot just a minute or two after leaving. I purposely spooked him off again, and again he returned within a couple of minutes.

Continuing on, I found a discarded spiral of tangled fishing line and picked it up for the trash barrel. On a lark, I decided to try to catch that trout by tying the old ratty dirty fur bug on to that tangled line and hand-flinging it at the fish. I spent perhaps half an hour trying to get the fly to drift toward him before deciding what I really needed was a sinker.

Since the creek runs through the middle of town and is fished heavily by locals, you could usually find all manners of things dropped along the bank – rusty rooster tails, empty sandwich bags, foam worm cups – no sinkers that day, though. As I wandered off in defeat, I noticed a small corroded washer in the gravel of the parking area. I snatched it up and returned to the fish, tied the washer on, flung my fur bug at him, and caught myself a trout without the benefit of a rod. Tangled line, a torn up dirty fur bug, a rusty washer, hand-tossed by an 11-year-old. "Wow, that's a stupid fish" I remember thinking.

I eventually stopped telling that story because I got tired of people calling me a liar. As time went on, though, I came to the determination that people accused me of making up the tale for one simple reason: the story conflicted with their belief that trout are smart. In order to believe my story, they would have to accept that their struggles in catching trout had nothing to do with the trout's brain power; it had to do with their own.

There are many differences between humans and animals, of course. Interestingly enough, one of the most human of traits is our pridefulness. It's that lack of humility that prevents so many of us from intellectual growth. Humans tend to believe in the sanctity of certainty, but it's the lack of certainty that fuels invention. Think back to the great innovators of the modern age. In nearly every instance they were told by the establishment experts that their ideas would certainly not work.

In the early 1900s, Ransom Olds and Henry Ford were told they certainly couldn't manufacture cars fast enough to make them affordable for the masses. They weren't so certain, though, and between the two of them, the assembly line was invented. Bill Gates and Steve Jobs were both ridiculed at the notion that families could have computers in the home. The "experts" were certain, but Gates and Jobs were not. This uncertainty in the face of what logic seems to tell us is true is actually what it means to be a visionary. You might be tempted to argue with me here, to tell me that Gates and Jobs were certain they were right and the "experts" were wrong, but that's not the case. Like all entrepreneurs, they were taking a gamble. They were HOPING they were right, and it turns out they were. And today you probably have multiple computers in your home, office, car, and one in your pocket or even in your hand. Their belief in the future of home and mobile computing was real, but it wasn't what we'd call a "sacred" belief.

We all have sacred beliefs. I'm not talking about religion, although that's included. I'm talking about any belief that is non-negotiable. You believe something and there's nothing anyone can say that will convince you that you might have it wrong. In February of 2014, creationist Ken Ham and scientist Bill Nye debated the origins of the universe. The closing question was: what could get you to change your mind? Ken Ham's response was "nothing." Bill Nye's response was "evidence." Regardless of what you believe about the Biblical creation story, Bill Nye's attitude is the one that will lead to innovation.

That said, the most common sacred beliefs we indulge are generally related to ourselves: I'm smart, I'm strong, I'm a good judge of character, I'm a good person, I'm right. It's really tough to back away from those beliefs, even when we're faced with concrete evidence to the contrary. When we see evidence that contradicts a sacred belief, we experience what's called cognitive dissonance — lack of harmony in the mind.

Let's say you have the sacred belief that you're a dog lover. You post cute dog pictures on Facebook. You donate to the local shelter or rescue. Your favorite movie is "Marley and Me." Everyone would agree you are a verified dog lover. But today was a terrible no-good very bad day and when you got home your dog got excited and jumped on you, almost knocking you down. So you kicked him. Hard. He yelped and ran to hide under the bed. Hmmm... evidence contradicting that you're a "dog lover." You're now experiencing cognitive dissonance.

The logical response is to analyze your sacred belief: "am I REALLY a dog lover, or do I only love dogs when I'm in the right mood?" The emotional response, on the other hand, is to dismiss the contradicting evidence as false, add a new belief, or otherwise play mind games with yourself to protect the sacred belief. To completely protect your sacred belief you'd have to convince yourself you did not kick the dog. In this case, it's easier to add new beliefs. "The dog had it coming." "This was a good learning experience for the dog." "I have to be the pack leader." "Punishment is sometimes the best option for behavior modification." "Maybe I overreacted, but it was still the right choice."

There's a saying that has stuck with me for some time. I wish I knew who said it first because it's brilliant in its simplicity. "It's impossible to have an intelligent conversation with someone unless you can first admit you might be wrong." Notice that's talking about YOU — not the other guy. Dale Carnegie said, "Nine times out of ten, an argument ends with each of the contestants more firmly convinced than ever that he is absolutely right." My gut tells me the odds are even worse than that. In study after study, when participants are asked to rate their own intelligence on a scale from 0-10, where 5 would be average, the average score people give themselves is 7. Think about that for a second. And in 1977, a study found 94 percent of college professors rated themselves above average in comparison to their college professor colleagues.

If you and I have a disagreement you might make a good point in our argument. But if I can't admit that I might be wrong (sacred belief), then the only other option is that you're a liar or an idiot. Now add Facebook and stir. Lifelong friendships end and family members are alienated. Of course, the topics are usually politics or religion, but people can be passionate about trout, too, which is why they would rather assume my story about the stupid trout and the fur bug is a lie. That's easier to accept than admitting they're wrong about trout being smart, which, by the way, is the false belief introduced to protect another sacred belief ("I'm a good fisherman") when faced with contradictory evidence ("I'm not catching very many trout").

Just as the phrase "It's Not About You" has jump-started the spiritual journey of many, the phrase "Trout Are Stupid" needs to direct your journey as a trout hunter. The brain of a rainbow trout is BB-sized, after all. Please don't send me argumentative emails about this assertion. I can see them now: "You said in your book that trout brains are the size of a BB, but I should point out that they are actually the size of a small pea. If you can't get that right, how can I trust anything you say?" Thank you, Mr. Wizard.

The point is, a trout's brain does not allow for higher functions. Higher brain activity like creativity and multi-stage problem-solving almost entirely takes place in the cerebral cortex — the gray wrinkly outer part of the brain that you probably picture when someone says the word "brain." One step below the cerebral cortex on the brain-power scale is the basal ganglia — a collection of smaller structures in the brain that appear to be more involved in learning from experience and the trial-and-error style of decision-making. And one step lower on the functioning scale is the cerebellum, which is mostly geared to physical coordination and complex movement.

As you can imagine, a trout's cerebellum is well developed, as evidenced by their exceptional physical abilities. And while the basal ganglia part of its brain is not as well-developed as a mammal's, it's in fairly decent shape. It's that portion of the brain that enables them to recognize food choices, predators, mating behaviors, etc.

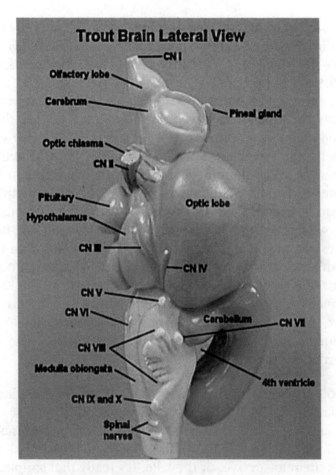

Trout Brain Lateral View

What may come as a surprise, however, is that a trout doesn't have a cerebral cortex at all. In the photo, you'll notice a variety of structures, but absolutely none of the gray wrinkly stuff you might expect. So, what exactly does that mean? Even the scientists are not 100% certain of what each sliver of the brain actually does, but what they do know is compelling. I have no interest in writing a textbook, but this information is the foundation of everything else to come, so bear with me here. When we talk about solving problems, what we're hoping to see is multi-stage problem-solving. Single-stage would refer to reactions like "I'm hungry, therefore I eat." Multi-stage problem-solving essentially takes the following form: (1) Recognize there's a problem; (2) Define the problem; (3) Identify a list of possible causes; (4) Identify a list of possible solutions to address each cause; (5) Begin choosing the most logical possible solutions from your list until the problem is solved. Obviously, humans do this, depending on how complex the problem is. We've also seen this behavior in primates, of course. In fact, we've seen this behavior in many mammals. It appears the mammalian cerebral cortex essentially develops a list of possible actions, categorizing them according to risk/reward comparisons. Since we know animals without a cerebral cortex (fish, birds, reptiles) do engage in decision-making, it's possible that the human basal ganglia are helping to choose an action from our list of possible solutions, but there's no real way to know. But since decision-making is possible without a cerebral cortex, the real question is, where is the list of possible solutions being developed if not in the gray matter? The short answer is: it isn't.

Without a cerebral cortex, their trouty decisions take place without any intellectual consideration of options or consequences. They are almost entirely reactive creatures (note I said "almost"). They either engage in behavior that allows them to survive, or they die. It's really that simple. Over time, their behaviors can change, but lasting changes are not due to education or comprehension. In fact, an "educated" trout is simply one that remembers and repeats the behaviors that bring reward and certainly do not cause anxiety or pain. Many consider those behavioral changes and patterns "instinctual," but even instincts don't exist in the way most people think.

I believe every "instinctual" behavior makes perfect sense. Before I explain this further, I need to clarify something. "Instinctual" behaviors are generally considered to be lower level brain function behaviors. Higher level brain activity (that activity taking place in the cerebral cortex) can override those lower brain impulses with a bit of effort. But without a cerebral cortex, the impulse can only be tempered by the basal ganglia, and that ability only develops through life experience. When the reactive impulse is not dampened by the suspicion created by life experience, you catch that fish!

Higher brain functions, what many consider to be "human" behaviors, are noticeably present in most mammals, just as we humans engage in the lower "instinctual behaviors." For example, some animals are very good at creative problem-solving. Have you ever tried to keep the squirrels out of your bird feeder? Some animals can experience very complex emotional states — apes, dolphins, and elephants, for example. And don't tell me my dog doesn't love me. He totally loves me. By contrast, humans are also very good at "instinctual" behaviors, but, in reality, these behaviors are simply involuntary, reactive or hormone-driven. For example, is breathing instinctual? If I threw a rock at your head, would ducking out of the way be considered an instinct? What about sexual urges?

Most behaviorists agree that the "fight or flight" response is instinctive or at least reactive, but either way, it makes a case that the basic "emotions" of fear and aggression are animalistic in nature. And my assertion here is that trout basically have three behaviors related to three basic emotional states: relaxed, afraid and aggressive. Everything a trout does will fall into one of those three categories. Well... okay, four categories, if you include horny.

Ducks and geese are also stupid. Even so, they are amazing creatures and animal behaviorists have long argued over their migration activities. What triggers the migration? Why do they so often follow essentially the same routes and end up in essentially the same places year after year? There's certainly been plenty of research into migratory bird behavior, and theories abound. A songbird may migrate at night, for example. Are they actively trying to avoid daytime predators? Are they using the stars for navigation? Is there any way we can ever know for sure?

Some biologists chalk it up to instincts and evolution and they're willing to leave it at that. But if you put yourself in the bird's place, the behaviors seem more logical than magical.

At the risk of over-simplifying things, imagine you're a duck. You wake up in the morning and make a simple decision. Do you stay here or do you go somewhere else? If you feel uncomfortable (too cold or too warm), you'll take flight and move off. But how is it that you know which direction to fly? Well, you don't. Not really. You're just a bird and you're not that much smarter than a trout, after all. You simply fly the direction the wind is blowing because it's the path of least resistance. Colder winds generally blow from the north to the south, so cold ducks fly somewhat southward. Warmer winds are usually blowing mostly north, so warm ducks fly mostly north.

If you live in one of the waterfowl migration lanes, you've probably noticed the geese and ducks flying north one day and south the next, right? In fact, you've probably seen confused ducks heading east or west as well. For the most part, they're flying with the wind, thermals, or that day's weather front. If anything pushes them to lean into the wind a bit, it will be their desire to follow the topography for one reason or another.

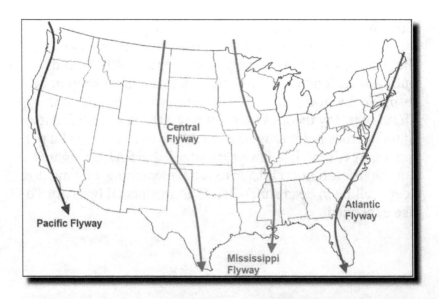

The coastal flyways, for example, roughly mirror the coasts. The central flyway generally follows the Rockies and the Missouri River valley, at least for a while. Of course, the Mississippi Flyway is easy to track. Aside from a preference for seeing familiar sights in general, keeping a wet and/or sheltered habitat within view, and a desire to group up with their buddies, they're mostly following weather patterns. And those patterns will eventually lead them back to the same general location year after year. This makes perfect sense, doesn't it? So, is this behavior instinctual? A more accurate description might be "accidental." There are repeating patterns in all the lower animal behaviors. If you can identify the patterns, you can predict the animal.

From the age of 9, I've been obsessed with figuring out the trout. I've read book after book and talked to more biologists, fishing guides and fly shop owners than I can remember. The most important bit of knowledge I discovered through these pursuits is that most experts don't REALLY know why trout do what they do. So, I set out to learn and discover what I could on my own.

To that end, I've become quite a research junky. A good amount of the information you'll read here are my own theories, based on my personal experience and field study, but I always look for the research that will either support or disprove my own beliefs. I hate being wrong, but I'm not afraid of it. My theories may not be 100% on the nose, but as of today, they seem to work pretty darn well. Perhaps I'll put out a new edition in a few years after I've REALLY figured out the trout. If not, I'll have to start researching why my dog keeps rolling in dead stuff. That is an instinctual behavior I'd like explained!

CHAPTER ONE

Figuring Out The Trout

As a college freshman, I was appalled to discover that I'd be required to take a class called "How to Study in College." How insulting! I had graduated from high school mostly with A's and B's so of course, I already knew how to study! As it turns out, however, it was the best educational experience I'd had to that point and I continue to utilize those lessons. The first lesson I learned was to assume my assumptions are wrong. In other words, I had to accept I didn't really know anything yet.

Of course, you already know that trout are soft-rayed fish restricted to waters where the water temperature doesn't generally move much above 70 degrees in the hottest part of the summer. Aside from that — and please forgive my supposition — much of what you know just ain't so. You will likely recognize some of these trout myths as false, but don't be surprised if you have a hard time accepting some of what I'll be describing to you.

I hear arguments supporting these trout myths all the time. The problem is that the arguments in favor of the myths are generally anecdotal in nature, whereas the evidence to the contrary is generally more scientific in nature. So, for the sake of future discussion, be prepared to fearlessly analyze your sacred trout-related beliefs.

First off, if you really want to "be the trout" and figure out what they're doing and why they're doing it, you should completely bury the notion of "instincts." If you're like most of us, you've equated instincts with some sort of magical Mother Nature-style influence over the wild. Even wildlife biologists will confidently proclaim "instincts" as a behavioral cause when the actual cause eludes them. If you can, burn into your mind that all behaviors make perfect sense and it's simply up to you to figure it out. Until you actually figure out what's causing the behavior in question, you'll never be able to truly anticipate that behavior. You may be able to guess that your local trout population will migrate upstream around the same time of year every year, or that certain flies will work best in certain seasons, but if you don't know why it happens, it's still a crapshoot.

It's been many years since I first started venturing into the world of guiding fishing trips. I had a few streams that I was very much in love with at the time and did my best to learn those trout inside and out. On one particular stream, I was surprised that a normally reliable stretch of the river seemed devoid of trout. I couldn't see anything and the action was non-existent. Rather than give up and go home, which was my normal behavior pattern at that time, I was feeling stubborn. So I decided that the trout had to be somewhere and I was going to find them, by God! I hoofed back to my hatchback and unfolded a small map of the creek to plan my attack.

I was already very familiar with this map but assumed I must be overlooking something. One thing that struck me was that the regulations did not just cover the traditional trout-holding portion of the creek. The highlighted area that represented the state's trout management area also extended well upstream of the first primary spring, well downstream of where I'd ever caught a trout and also up a few tributaries that I'd never fished before. Hmm… those state guys must know something.

To make a long story short, I discovered some fantastic fishing in a part of the river that, according to traditional wisdom, was not supposed to hold trout. I chose that area on a hunch and boy, did my hunch pay off. Upon finding the fish, I began getting solid hits on perhaps 75% of my drifts, hooking dozens of decent fish in a matter of a few hours. This shocking discovery provided fantasy fishing for a month or so, and it was great while it lasted. The next year the same results were found in the same location in the same season. Aha! It wasn't a fluke! The third year — the year I started guiding my first few clients — I took a fisherman to that same area during the "correct" time of year. Guess what? No fish.

It was certainly frustrating and more than a bit embarrassing. I figured the fish were just a bit late in arriving, so I kept trying. After a while, though, I finally had to accept that they weren't coming at all. Something had changed, but I didn't know what. I had thrown the dice and rolled snake eyes, even though I was absolutely certain of my system. Truth is, I didn't have a system — I'd simply identified a short-term trend.

As hard as it was for my ego, I had to accept that I had not yet figured out those trout. I decided right then that this would be my goal, so I began collecting data. I chose three rivers and made a personal commitment to fish them equally in rotation, fishing as much as 15 days in a month.

Initially, I only documented where I fished, the time of day, weather, and successful flies and methods. Eventually, I began seining the river to survey insect populations and also began documenting water temperature. I learned about dissolved oxygen, and, not knowing how to take an actual measurement, began to document rainfall and air temperatures to categorize oxygen levels as "poor," "fair," "good," or "excellent." Finally, I began to take visual surveys (snorkeling) to document the trout I saw, the behaviors I observed, locations, concentrations of fish, etc. To this day, I carry a pair of goggles in my fishing vest in case I get bored with fishing. I also conducted experiments and read research papers to verify or debunk as many trout myths as I could. For example, do trout REALLY have such good eyesight that they can see 4-pound test fishing line under water? I'll bet you have an opinion on that one.

CHAPTER TWO

Trout Folklore

My trout addiction started fairly early in life. My family had moved to Waynesville, Missouri the summer before my 4th-grade year and it took no time at all to discover the spring-fed river that ran through the center of town. Of course, I had to fish the creek. Generally, I threw worms and caught a variety of panfish. I noticed other people fishing as well, but I didn't give them much attention. In truth, I was more interested in wading and swimming and jumping from the retaining wall that kept the gravel road from slipping into the spring pool.

During one fateful summertime walk to the creek, I came across a strange scene. Every possible place that one might park a car had a car parked in it. Crowds of fishermen lined the creek, many struggling to untangle their line from the line of another fisherman. To my eyes, it looked stressful rather than enjoyable. As I walked closer to the bank, I noticed the occasional fisherman rapidly reel in a fish, drop it into a bucket or basket or thread it onto a stringer, and quickly re-rig to cast back out. What in the world was going on? Of course, I was too shy to ask. I would simply have to linger, observe and eavesdrop.

When a man a few feet from me caught a rainbow trout, I was stunned. I'd never before seen a fish like this. It was bigger than anything I'd ever caught — about a foot long — and it was covered from top to bottom and from one end to the other with a dense splatter of black spots. But in addition to this, there were forest greens and mustard yellows, and where the pinks and reds and blues overlapped, there were violets and purples and silver flashes that were only evident when the sun hit it just right. What a fish.

You can probably guess that I stumbled upon our local version of the "stocking truck trout derby." With the creek running through the middle of town, there was no way a hatchery truck could be hidden from the local fishermen, and so a sort of monthly ritual had developed. The Missouri Department of Conservation would dump in five or six hundred fish and a crowd of fishermen would arrive to pull 90% of them back out. The next stocking day I was there too, but I didn't catch anything. Indeed, it took a great deal of time and effort (mostly observing and eavesdropping) before I began to piece together what I was doing wrong.

Of course, catching those recently stocked trout is not as difficult as, say, catching a stream-bred fish with a few years of life experience dodging otters, herons, and fishermen. Even so, most folks discover that using typical warm-water panfish/catfish techniques doesn't work very well on trout. You certainly might catch a trout on a shad side under a bobber, trout being stupid after all. But to catch any quantity of them (hatchery trout included) you need to adjust your tactics.

What I soon learned as a youngster is that you'll have better luck using a small hook that can be hidden within a single salmon egg or kernel of corn rather than by stringing seven or eight pieces onto a long-shanked hook. I believed this was due to their reputation for "being picky." It's what I'd heard from other fishermen, so I accepted it as fact. "Trout simply don't like to eat big stuff," I thought.

I also surmised that you "must" use the thinnest fishing line you can find if you want to have any luck at all. These ideas were spoon-fed to me by older and wiser fishermen and it was easy to convince me that trout must have fantastic eyesight. Of course, they must be able to see my fishing line. That explains why I'm not catching anything. Would I bite into a cheeseburger if there were a piece of string hanging from it leading to the nearest lake? I should say not!

The third thing I was able to figure out was how to artificially recreate the same type of feeding frenzy I often witnessed shortly after the stocking truck left — by chumming of course. By flinging out a fist full of corn and then casting my corn-baited hook into the midst of it, I was sure to get a bite on nearly every cast. How exciting!

With these three new bits of knowledge, I quickly became what I considered to be a skilled trout fisherman, especially for a fourth grader. Naturally, I was a bit horrified when an adult fisherman chastised me for chumming – apparently, it was bad form. And I must admit how disappointing it was to discover that I was not nearly the gifted fisherman I considered myself to be after removing chumming from my bag of tricks.

Even at the age of 9, trout mythology had begun appearing and taking root. The first two things I learned about rainbow trout were at best only marginally accurate. I held them to be true simply because it made sense in a warm-blooded land-loving air-breathing sort of way. The reality is, they were and remain to this day two of the most fervently believed trout-related myths.

Now, it is actually true that rainbow trout do often eat smaller bites and it is true that thinner line generally works better than thicker line. Even so, the root of the truth in both cases does not lie in their instincts or even in their eyesight.

CHAPTER THREE

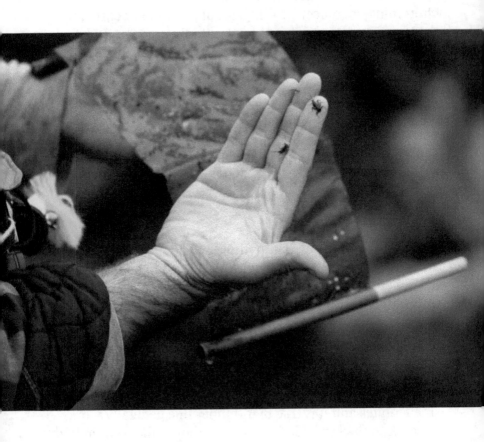

Picky Eaters?

Fish story: Trout are picky. Bass will eat just about anything, but a trout is fussy about its diet. An "educated" trout only likes small baits or flies that are exact replicas of the real thing. If your bait doesn't look just right, they just won't bite.

If you've done much trout fishing then you're probably already aware of some of the flaws in this belief. In fact, I'll bet you're aware of the relatively new fad of throwing multi-hook streamers as big as your shoe or flies made from mop parts. But, just in case...

Soft-rayed fish like trout tend to have smaller mouths than similarly-sized spiny-rayed predator fish like bass, which should lead you to the simple conclusion that they tend to eat smaller bites — a smaller mouth means a smaller mouthful. Things get a bit more complicated than that, but it is a good starting point.

Since bass have the ability to ingest larger prey, it means that they are able to ingest more calories with every mouthful. This is one reason why bass often feed more aggressively than trout and other soft-rayed fish. They can afford to burn 30 calories chasing down a crayfish because they're going to absorb 60 calories when they eat it. If a trout has a taste for crayfish, he won't be able to choke down the 60-calorie variety, simply because it's too big. Therefore, he may have to settle for a 20-calorie version. If that's the case, can he afford to burn 30 calories to chase it down?

Any animal that makes a habit of burning 30 calories to catch a 20-calorie meal is going to starve. Successful trout will notice drifting bugs even before their yolk sacs are absorbed, so they learn how to feed successfully and lazily right off the bat. And even most hatchery trout will notice bugs drifting by and will learn to feed this way within a couple of weeks of stocking, but a smaller group of those same hatchery fish will literally starve themselves to death by chasing prey all over the river. Even so, don't assume that it's a matter of intellect. It's more a matter of luck and, to a lesser degree, it's a matter of duplicating the behaviors they see other trout engaging in. Yes, they do that.

The act of eating at restaurants has always fascinated me. Of course, it makes perfect sense if you're traveling and have no kitchen to cook your own meal. But why do we leave our homes with food in our refrigerators and pantries and go to a restaurant? One reason is the quality of the food we can obtain. Everyone likes to be pampered, so it's understandable that we'd be willing to get in the car and drive across town for the occasional $50 filet mignon or a lobster dinner. But that's not what I'm talking about here. I'm talking about those times when we hit that mediocre $8 Chinese buffet. And what about those times when you visit the drive-through lane for a bag of room temperature tacos? At the risk of sounding judgmental, it's a combination of being spoiled and lazy. We're too lazy to cook so we pay someone else to do it for us. And we're spoiled so, of course, we demand to be fed immediately when we're hungry. If we can get someone to deliver it, even better! In that way, most animals, including humans and trout, are quite similar to each other.

Even though trout also like to treat themselves to that occasional $50 filet, they're almost always lazy in their dietary practices. Simply speaking, when a trout with a little life experience notices bits of things drifting past him in the current, he's going to taste some of it. In fact, most of the time, a fish feeding opportunistically will taste anything that looks like a potential meal. This doesn't mean that they'll actually eat bits of leaves and sticks drifting by, although it's not unheard of. We're just talking about a taste. The anatomy of a trout's mouth is what makes this possible.

Not only is a trout's mouth smaller than that of a bass, it's also meatier. This additional tissue includes a more concentrated tangle of nerve endings, meaning they can tell by touch or by taste if something is edible within milliseconds. If they see something drifting by that looks edible, into the mouth it will often go. If it feels squishy and tastes good, down the hatch it slides. If not, it pops back out of that fish's mouth almost immediately. Sometimes he'll spit it out because the taste or smell is surprising — garlic flavored dough bait or a piece of meat from a decomposing animal, for example — but he won't necessarily abandon it right off. He may taste it over and over, even breaking it up into smaller bites before actually swallowing it. This taste-test activity is a common feeding behavior for the average-sized trout.

There are a few exceptions to the laziness rule. Trout will pursue prey, of course. But since this action burns calories like they're going out of style, the conditions and the potential payoff have to be right. Most humans don't go out for that $50 filet mignon as a matter of habit. It's more of a special occasion and the same is true for trout. You'll only pay that kind of money for a meal if it truly is top quality. Even so, there's still a limit to how far you're willing to drive and how much you're willing to spend. Similarly, trout are only triggered to pursue prey under certain circumstances, and even then, there will be a limit to how far they're willing to travel. But there are wildcards that can change the algorithm. Perhaps you have a coupon for that legendary steakhouse, or perhaps they have a special going on this weekend, or maybe you received a gift certificate as a birthday present, or maybe you're rich and have money to burn. Those instances might change how far you're willing to drive or how frequently you'd be willing to make the trip, right?

Obviously, a trout that eats something big is in a more aggressive mood. The good news is that it's easy to identify what triggers an aggressive mood and when those conditions are present, you can adjust your tactics to improve your success rate. That said, the only real condition required to prompt the DESIRE to eat large prey is hunger. When a trout is hungrier than normal, he'll be more interested in larger-than-normal bites of food. Since fish are cold-blooded, their metabolism is directly tied to their body temperature. This means warmer water will increase their metabolism, which means warmer water makes a fish hungrier. It's the warmest time of the year when trout will actively feed on the largest food it can grab. This is one reason size 8 grasshopper patterns can be so successful in the middle of August. Grasshoppers are available earlier and later, but it's during the dog days of summer when most hopper action happens. It's also the reason you should try giant nymphs drifted slow and deep, or great big streamers slowly twitched along in the current at this time of year.

You've no doubt seen the images of salmon swimming upstream through crowds of bears trying to snatch them from the water, tearing them limb from limb (yes, I know fish don't have limbs). Trust me when I say those salmon are nervous. And yet they continue doing what they have to do.

Trout react in a similar fashion. If a trout is hanging out minding his own business and a fisherman comes stomping over while throwing a fly at him, is he going to stop eating? Maybe. If the river in question sees very few fishermen, that fish will simply take off or hunker down until the intruder leaves. BUT, if that trout sees fishermen all the time, day in and day out, he MUST continue to eat in spite of his nervousness; otherwise, he's not going to make it. And so the trout begins feeding in a style that makes him appear picky.

If you've ever fished at a heavily pressured over-stocked trout fishery crowded with several hundred of your closest friends (we have four heavily stocked state-managed trout parks and a very popular tailwater here in Missouri, for example), then you've probably been infuriated by a trout that will approach your fly, almost touching it with his nose, before turning away. Those trout are resident trout, meaning they've been living in the stream long enough to have grown suspicious of their food, usually through the experience of taking someone's bait and either escaping or being returned to the water by the fisherman. So, when something else that looks like food drifts to him, he'll take an extra moment before deciding whether to taste it (and for the record, he's sniffing it, not staring at it). He's not technically looking for a reason to reject it, mind you — that would suggest problem-solving intellect. But he's also not as interested in tasting things he doesn't immediately recognize.

When a real bug drifts to him, it always looks like a bug, acts like a bug, and smells like a bug, and it will almost never be rejected. The difference between this pressured trout and trout in wilder settings is that this irritating trout is less likely to feed curiously, randomly tasting things like sticks, a bit of leaf, or your goofy-looking yarn fly. He'll only taste something if it already appears to be food, if he's not 100%

certain, that taste test will be lightning fast. That's not being picky, exactly, but it is a behavioral adaptation to living in a heavily fished environment. I've said "nervous" previously, but I doubt that literal nervousness plays into it. Trout are easily startled, which engages their flight response, but they just don't have the brain power to experience anxiety as a human would understand it.

 If you've ever fished crowded trout waters like portions of the San Juan, the Frying Pan, the White River tailwater system, or any of the privately-owned trout ranches or state-funded trout parks like we have in Missouri, you've seen it firsthand. If you can overcome their nervousness with your technique, your results in less-trafficked wilder trout streams where trout are generally more relaxed will make you feel like a trout fishing genius! Of course, that's not to say fish don't have their favorite foods, though — at least in a manner of speaking.

Given the option, every animal will develop "preferences." I put that word in quotes because I'm planning to tear the word apart shortly. The goldfinches in my backyard prefer thistle over millet. That's a notable observation because a bird's brain and intellect, such as it is, has much in common with that of a fish. Even though the cerebral cortex is missing, they can remember what works for them and they will certainly repeat behaviors that produce a desirable outcome, but that's not why they "prefer" thistle. They're designed to eat it. Their beaks are equipped for splitting that specific seed. It also apparently tastes good.

In the same way, once an inexperienced trout gets a taste for insects, crustaceans, and little fish, they start preferring that type of food source over, say, hatchery pellets or dough bait. This isn't due to one tasting better than the other. It's more a matter of availability and success. Drilling down even further, that trout might also develop a preference for little fish rather than bugs, or perhaps he's had more success eating dark brown insects than the other available colors. That said, it's not "preference" in the human sense of the word. This isn't the old "do you prefer chocolate or strawberry ice cream" sort of thing. They prefer the foods that are more available to them, that they're more successful catching, that they're designed to eat, and that have a lot of calories. In other words, a trout will almost always prefer the biggest bite of food they can easily swallow with the smallest amount of effort. And, yes, there are exceptions.

A hatchery-raised trout that survives his first few days in a heavily fished river quickly realizes that dough bait, salmon eggs, and spinners are not to be trusted as menu options — they hurt your mouth. This trial by fire simply accelerates his conversion to preferring bugs, because while he develops wariness related to eating bait, he'll be actively looking for alternative food sources. So, in a matter of just a few days, he'll begin tasting drifting insects and a new feeding behavior begins to emerge. However, if he chases what he thinks is a bug that drifts or swims away in an unnatural manner and feels a hook, he'll learn a new lesson. Only food options that behave a certain way can be trusted.

Since trout are only able to learn in a linear fashion (no cerebral cortex), it means they don't have the ability to apply multiple layers of qualifiers. In other words, they don't have the brains to say to themselves: "it must look like this" + "it must behave like this" + "it must smell like this" + "it must taste like this." Although they'll test their food choices using all four qualifiers at various times, their mental capabilities can really only handle one or two specific qualifiers at a time, and the number one qualifier will almost always be the fly's behavior rather than the fly pattern itself. And the more often they attack something that behaves outside of those parameters, get hooked and survive, the more that lesson is reinforced.

Over the years, I've had the overwhelming pleasure of watching countless skeptical clients hook into whopper fish on silly flies I tied onto their tippets — Chernobyl Ants, Y2K Bugs, Mohair Leeches, Girdle Bugs, etc. And I'm not talking about brood stock fish that were dumped in the river yesterday. I'm talking about fish that have lived in the river for several years, feeding naturally and learning how to survive. Those clients I speak of all had one thing in common. They could cast, and they knew how to mend their line to achieve a natural drift. In other words, an experienced trout may learn a number of different lessons during his life: "no garlic smell," "no yellow," "no spinners," "bugs only," etc. But in every case one lesson is consistent — real food BEHAVES like real food. That means an experienced resident fish will often ignore those other lessons, as long as the potential snack behaves naturally. This isn't always the case, of course. When a popular river suddenly gets the reputation for being a "streamer river," for example, it won't take long for the fish to learn to avoid Wooly Buggers. But, once the fishermen ease off of that fly and start using other techniques, the lesson of proper food behavior becomes dominant once again. And that is why some of the largest trout ever caught have been caught on silly baits.

Bottom line: we're not talking about being picky. We're talking about a trout finding its comfort zone, and the most important aspect of that comfort zone for a resident fish is the behavior of the food rather than its appearance. However, there is such a thing as being "selective" and it happens to ALL fish at times. Truthfully speaking, though, it's the exception to the rule of daily feeding behaviors.

If you've ever had teenagers mooching off you, then you'll find this example to be very familiar. Sit a 14-year-old boy in front of the TV and hand him a family-size bag of potato chips. What happens? He sits there staring at the TV and unconsciously devours that entire bag of chips, doesn't he? If you offer him something comparable but different (cheese puffs, for example), his response will generally be "Nah, I'm good." You'll have to offer him something that's more highly prized to really catch his attention – perhaps a bag of M&M's. Even in that case, you might have to throw it at him to snap him out of his stupor. This boy is engaged in "zoned-out comfort zone feeding," just like a selective trout.

So, let's be clear. Selective feeding refers to a trout only eating a specific bug and refusing all others, which generally happens during a hatch. I've been guilty of describing it as a fish demanding the exact right bug in the exact right size, the exact right color, the exact right spot, demonstrating the exact right behavior, but I have to admit that's hyperbole. If you'll recall, I previously mentioned that trout only have the brain power to keep one or two qualifiers in mind when feeding. This is a two-qualifier event — appearance and behavior. It's really not so complicated once you understand what's going on.

When a hatch begins, the nymphs in question start climbing out of the rocks, vegetation or silt where they live the majority of their lives. Different bugs do different things at this point, but the traditionally recognized hatching mayfly will kick off into the current and start swimming toward the surface as they drift downstream. When these bugs begin to appear en masse, the trout will gradually recognize them as real food, feeding on these drifting and swimming nymphs. If you happen to be nymph fishing with a fly of the approximate size and color of the natural bug, you can really tear them up at this stage of the game. As the hatch progresses, the trout will follow this activity from the bottom of the creek to the surface as more and more of the bugs are moving in that direction. A fisherman allowing his fly to swing out below him at the end of the drift will often hook into some of the trout keying in on those upward swimming nymphs.

Those nymphs that reach the surface will either begin breaking out of their skins in an effort to "hatch" into their adult form, or they'll swim back down toward the streambed. Trout feeding on the emerging nymphs will produce dimples in the water's surface but rarely breaks in the film. The successful fisherman will be the one who casts an appropriate unweighted emerger pattern at this point. And as the bugs begin to climb out of their husks, the appropriate parachute pattern will work well. Before long, though, they'll switch to feeding on hatching adults, which will be best imitated with an appropriate dry fly. If this specific hatch has been repeating for a few days, the adult version of the dry fly can work well, as the insects return to the water to drop their eggs. And, finally, the spent-wing pattern can pull some fish as those egg-laying adults give up the ghost. Simple, right?

Sometimes, the whole thing takes just a couple of hours and most fishermen struggle to figure out what's going on. "I can see they're feeding on something, but I don't know what it is." And while they randomly start tying on every fly in the box, the chance that they'll accidentally stumble upon the right fly at the right moment is really slim. But your chances improve if you understand the process for what it is.

When the magic hatch begins, the trout may have been eating their normal diet all day: scud, the occasional nymph, an ant here and there, maybe a minnow that wasn't paying attention. And then, Mother Nature sits them on the couch in front of the TV and gives them a bag of chips. The sheer quantity of this one specific type of food simply gets their attention. When you drift a scud through that cloud of hatching bugs, the trout may or may not even notice it, because he's "zoned out" and is simply focused on "chips" for now. They all look alike and they all behave the same way. After eating a few of them without anything bad happening, the trout's "comfort zone" begins to reshape. The lesson he's learned is that this food is safe to eat, meaning his nervousness and anxiety related to feeding essentially disappears.

As the nymphs stop drifting and start swimming, Mr. Trout just follows the action upward and his comfort zone adjusts to accommodate. And as the emerging bugs begin to move to the top of the water column, so do the fish. Once the hatch has gone full circle, unfortunately, you have a bunch of fish with full tummies and the level of feeding on other food items is now anything but aggressive. And that is why we don't let our teenagers eat a giant bag of chips right before dinner.

On most trout streams, insect hatches occur with seasonal regularity on a fairly predictable daily schedule. But some hatches are better than others and hatches certainly don't happen around the clock. And while trout are typically selective during those hatches, the premise that trout are naturally "picky" is no more accurate than saying your teenager is picky because he refuses cheese puffs while eating potato chips. To be a successful fisherman during these selective times, you just need some inside information. Doing your homework to learn about local hatches is a great way to start. You can also seine the creek bottom to look at the bugs to determine for yourself what eventualities you need to be prepared for. If you are fishing a stream that has MASSIVE midge hatches, for example, there will be times when the trout key in on midges exclusively and fearlessly.

You just need to identify which brand of chips that teenager is eating, so you can match the snack. That's easier said than done, but when you're prepared, and when you recognize what's happening and adjust your tactics accordingly, fishing a hatch properly does not feel like trying to catch "picky" trout. It feels more like catching "stupid" trout – trout feeding without fear. And it will almost seem like you can't do anything wrong.

On one trip to the Rockies, I hit the Frying Pan River during the green drake hatch completely by accident. The place was packed, but not many people were catching fish. I talked to several fishermen that first day and I discovered most of them were fishing traditional drake dries and mostly struggling and irritable, catching a fish here and there. One guy was fishing a dry with a nymph dropper and he reported periods of time without any action, but also periods of time when he couldn't keep the fish away, catching most of them on the dropper. This made the lightbulb come on for me and it forever changed the way I fish hatches. I quickly tied up a bunch of butt-ugly flies and had a great time. More on that later.

That was over 20 years ago, by the way, and the system I fell into that day has continued to prove effective. And I want to make this point as clear as I can. These were not good-looking flies. They were roughly about the right size and shape and color, but UGLY. By no measure could you claim I was "matching the hatch." The selling point was the behavior, even though the fish were feeding selectively. My flies were in the right location and were behaving appropriately. In other words, stop worrying so much over fly selection and focus your efforts on your technique.

CHAPTER FOUR

A $50 Filet

Fish story: Trout like cold water — the colder the better.

I hate to break it to you, but trout do not care one bit what the water temperature is. I know, I know. It shocked me, too. And the idea that they swim upstream looking for the spring or the melting snowpack is just plain silly. Trout are stupid if you'll recall. Their entire world is basically the 15-foot wide sphere that surrounds them right at this moment. They don't know what a spring is, where it is, or why they should go there. If they feel good, then life is sweet. Period. Regarding trout "liking" cold water, it turns out fish are cold-blooded. This means that their body temperatures adjust to match their surroundings. So, if the water is 40 degrees, the trout's body temperature is 40 degrees. If the water is at 75, so is the fish. Warm-blooded animals register comfort and discomfort regarding body temperature, but cold-blooded animals do not. The temperature change does alter their body systems, though, and it affects fish in two very notable ways.

I had a buddy once who was spending some time outdoors with his little girl on an unseasonably warm winter's day. On a concrete wall, he noticed a small lizard basking in the sun and he thought it would be nice to catch it to show to his daughter up close — I believe she was two years old at the time. Carefully, he crept up on the lizard, slowly putting his hand on the concrete wall. He anticipated the lizard would dart away like a bolt of lightning (in fact, he was surprised that the lizard hadn't run off already), so he tensed himself to strike and swung his hand as quickly as he could toward the lizard. The lizard never even blinked and my buddy smeared its little body along the concrete to his own horror and the cries of his daughter. It hadn't occurred to him that the lizard's body temperature was probably only about 50 degrees, meaning his blood pressure and his heart rate were down, dulling his mental and physical reaction time. It also means my buddy could have walked over to him, reached out and picked him up without any problem at all. HOWEVER, if he'd tried to catch this lizard in August on a 98-degree day, there's not a chance in a million that he ever would have gotten close.

Since trout are also cold-blooded, the same is true for them. The colder the water, the lower their heart rate and blood pressure, the slower their reaction time, and the lower their ability to manipulate their muscles. Another piece of the puzzle you may find interesting is that cold-blooded animals burn fewer calories as they get colder, meaning they are less hungry. "Cold" equals "slow metabolism." I'm sure you're familiar with that term. I personally struggle a bit with my weight 100% due to my lower than average metabolism (shut up). And we all know people who can eat whatever they want without gaining a pound, simply because they have such a high metabolism (bastards). Of course, we'll not discuss the fact that I'm partial to pastries and that those skinny minis do crazy things like eating vegetables and lifting weights and running and other things that hurt.

There is a flip side to this water temperature coin, however. As the water warms, the trout's metabolism goes up. This includes a higher heart rate and higher blood pressure while burning more calories. In other words, THEY ARE HUNGRIER! The warmer the water, the more they have to eat to survive. I know what you're saying. If that's really true, then why do they only live in cold-water environments? If they're so hungry, why is trout fishing during the dog days of summer often tough? You see, water temperature is closely related to something else trout need to survive: oxygen.

Water temperature and the water's carrying capacity for dissolved oxygen (the O2 molecules trapped between the H2O molecules) are inversely related. That means, as one goes up, the other goes down. In this case, temperature controls oxygen. Cold water can hold much more dissolved oxygen (D.O.) than warm water and as the water warms, the D.O. decreases. The next time you boil water on the stove, watch it closely. The first thing you'll notice is that little air bubbles begin to form on the bottom of the pan under the water. Eventually, those bubbles let loose and then more and more will begin to shoot to the surface. Once the water gets going, though, the bubbles will disappear. The water will begin to roll (i.e. "a rolling boil"), but the lack of air bubbles indicates that the dissolved oxygen has all been pushed out of the water by the application of heat. If you were then to remove the water from the heat and allow it to cool, it will gradually absorb oxygen from the air as it cools. The water will cool to room temperature and will eventually reach its maximum carrying capacity of D.O. for that temperature, although it will take quite some time. However, you could jump-start the absorption rate simply by grabbing a straw and blowing bubbles in the water like a kid at a restaurant blowing bubbles in his milk.

For the fisherman, this means that the water temperature thing is much more complex than most people realize. Colder is not simply better. Instead, think of water temperature and D.O. content as overlapping "zones" of productivity. Too cold and they're not hungry. Too warm and they have trouble breathing and can't pursue their prey as effectively. So, ideally, you want the water conditions to be like the porridge that Goldilocks picked — "just right." When it's not, you have to adjust your tactics.

In my local waters, when the water temperature dips below 45 degrees, the fish's metabolism really bottoms out, meaning they're just not hungry. This number will vary from region to region and water to water since trout are accustomed to their normal local conditions, but the principle remains the same. When the water gets "too cold," there's plenty of oxygen, but no appetite and slow muscle reaction time due to decreased blood flow. Do they eat? Yes, but not much. After stuffing down your Thanksgiving dinner, are you ready to wolf down a pizza? Probably not. What are you willing to eat at a time like that? Well, if it's exceptionally tempting (like my sister's Dixie Pecan Pie) or something traditional (like good old pumpkin pie with whipped cream), you'll probably try to make some room. Similarly, you'll need to offer a cold trout something that's exceptionally tempting that they'll eat because it's just a great opportunity (like a really buggy looking fly tied with flash and rubber legs) or something traditional that they'll eat out of habit (like an exact imitation of stuff they eat all the time). Even so, you have to remember their clumsy slow reaction time and do your best to drift those flies right to their nose.

When the water temp rises as springtime approaches, the trout will gradually start feeding more readily as their appetite improves. If you fish your local waters frequently, when you suddenly see improved feeding activity in late winter or early spring, you're probably still a few degrees away from the real magic. In much of the country, that magic water temperature is 55 degrees, but that varies quite a bit, depending on what your local trout population is accustomed to. Even so, when your river's magic temperature is reached, the water is already carrying close to the maximum amount of D.O. it will hold (it's been a long cold winter, after all, so D.O. has been high for months) and the fish are suddenly HUNGRY. Appetite plus energy equals fun! They'll begin to feel like a bunch of crazed high school football players chasing after cheerleaders and looking to get into fights. And as they begin to move upstream against the fluctuating currents associated with springtime rains, they'll eventually crowd into pools and will feed both aggressively and competitively. This is one of the "magical" migration times you've heard so much about.

My home river floods HARD. It's also very gravelly along the entire length of the trout-holding section, so appropriate spawning territory is available all over the place. And each year I find fish on redds (spawning beds). The thing is, the final location of most of the spawning activity varies over a wide range from year to year — like 5 or 6 miles. To me, that seems like proof that they are not migrating to reach spawning grounds. To me, it seems like migration followed by spawning are simply two behaviors happening in that order essentially by accident.

Regardless of the season or where they're located on the river, as long as the water temperature stays in the lower 60s, the trout will continue to enjoy good oxygen and an active metabolism. You'll catch them on streamers being stripped in like a minnow, drifting nymphs, and also on dries, emergers, wet flies, etc. Of course, not every fly will work all the time. You'll still need to figure that part out. Even so, if you hit the river when the conditions are right — perhaps in spring or even early summer when the highly oxygenated winter water warms into the magic zone — you're putting yourself in the best position to catch the highest number of fish, including some real whoppers.

As summer progresses, the water temperature will gradually rise, of course, and the decreasing oxygen content will start to affect the fish. If they pursue a bait fish or swim well outside of their normal lie to grab a drifting nymph, they'll discover they're a bit out of breath after the exertion. Once they hit this wall, you'll notice that streamer fishing dies down pretty quickly. You'll still catch a few fish stripping in streamers if you go REALLY slow, but you'll find that the best streamer action will come during the time of day when oxygen is highest (between 4:00 am and whenever the sun hits the water). Otherwise, you'll discover fish are becoming more lethargic, even as their metabolism continues to go up.

Once upon a time, I called a buddy who lived in Colorado to see about coming for a visit and some fishing. The only time I could do this was right before college classes resumed — the dreaded August trout fishing trip. He said he'd be happy to take me fishing but warned that we wouldn't catch any fish. "It's too hot." Even so, being the hard head that I am, I made the trip. He and I fished the Blue River and we fished traditional patterns in traditional sizes and colors using traditional techniques without luck. At the end of the third day of crappy fishing, I suggested we should mix things up a bit. By camp lantern light, we both tied flies that night. I tied up a wider variety of flies, including teeny tiny things, goofy attractors, grasshoppers in various sizes, and also a new stonefly-ish pattern tied much fatter than usual. To these stoneflies, I added a cluster of six or eight rubber legs that were really too long. Both of these rivers had decent stonefly populations averaging about an inch long, so that's the size I focused on. But I also tied some very small stoneflies and also some GREAT BIG ones. Seriously. We're talking twice as big as normal. These things looked like a mutant Amazon rainforest cockroach.

I caught a few on the grasshopper and had a thought. Are they eating the grasshopper because it's summer and grasshoppers are around? I'm sure that's part of it, but there are also aquatic insects around. So why grasshoppers and not pheasant tails? Is it a topwater thing? We didn't have any luck with elk hair caddis or other traditional dry flies. Hmm... Could it be the size?

I tied on one of my giant freaky-looking stoneflies in spite of my friend's teasing. Half an hour later, my buddy was using one of those flies himself. The night before, we were expecting day four to be the last day of fishing. We ended up staying until day seven and only left because the fall semester loomed large ahead of us both. We did sweat a lot and our campsite did not have showers, so we were stinking up the place. Interestingly, the mosquitos stopped biting us on day four — I'm guessing due to the stench. In spite of our discomfort and hygiene issues, we couldn't tear ourselves away. The fishing wasn't suddenly miraculous, but we were finally getting the results we wanted. We even caught a couple in the 20-inch category. We had discovered something important, but it took me a while to put it all together. It wasn't until I pieced together the whole cold-blooded, dissolved oxygen thing that I realized I could duplicate that success on those rivers year after year.

When the water temp rises into the upper 60s, the trout really begin to struggle. The oxygen content is low in most of the river, so they'll end up congregating in the best quality areas. Churning water with white caps adds oxygen to the water (just like the kid blowing bubbles in his milk), so deeper water with good shade downstream from white-capped riffles or a nice plunge will usually have the best local oxygen content, and you'll often find fish crowding together there. And guess what? The most dominant fish get the highest quality spots. If you can drift your fly to those spots, you've got a great chance at catching a dominant (aka BIG) fish. And, since the water is warm and their metabolism is up, these fish are very interested in anything that looks like it has a bunch of calories in it. That's one reason why big grasshoppers can work so well in the summer — lots of calories and they don't run away. And if you can get that great big nymph down to that super deep spot below the white caps, you've got gold, my friend.

Just like the whole town would scramble to cash in their free $50 filet mignon gift certificates at dinner time, there are two times each year when every fish in the river is given that "gift certificate." That gift certificate comes in the form of extremely high dissolved oxygen. Just like an exhausted athlete can regain his strength by sucking on an O2 tank on the sidelines, high dissolved oxygen gives trout amazing levels of endurance.

In the spring, when D.O. is crazy-high and the water temperature creeps high enough that they're feeling hungry, trout will swim across the whole darn river to grab your poorly tied brown wooly bugger, or anything else of size you throw at them. They may not be convinced that it's edible, but they're hungry, they're feeling good, and they can "afford the trip." And if you choose a fly or lure with some built-in components to help it look alive and swimmy — marabou, a rabbit strip, rubber legs, a heavy bead head, or maybe even a wobbly little crankbait — you're going to have some fun.

Bear in mind that, yes, they are hungry in the springtime, but they're not desperate for calories yet. They are actively feeding and gaining weight, but more normal-sized flies may at times work better than the stupid-huge flies I mentioned earlier. But take heart. In the heat of the summer, while they will not GO OUT for the $50 filet, they will love you for delivering it to them. If you were ravenously hungry and I brought you that $50 filet mignon and put it on your TV tray in front of you, would you refuse it? Of course not! Neither will they. Get that great big fly with tons of calories right on their TV tray and they will eat it. After all, they're starving, and they don't have any money for gas!

The second "gift certificate" season is autumn, although it's a bit more unpredictable. Wet cold fronts followed by wet warm fronts change the water conditions in ways that are too tough for us mere mortals to really follow. When the summer waters cool back into the lower 60s, the D.O. won't suddenly jump up. The water will gradually absorb oxygen on its own, and white caps and rainfall will add oxygen even more successfully, but that all takes some time. The magic moment you're hoping for is a nice late September or early October cold front with a steady cool rain. That's like having a few million kids blowing bubbles in their milk. That kind of event will get the trout feeling frisky. And if the rain is enough to swell the river a bit, they'll start swimming upstream and they'll start getting aggressive. And the kicker? They're still really darn hungry from a hard summer of warm low-oxygen water. So grab your rod and get your butt on the river before the next warm front screws it all up!

CHAPTER FIVE

Monofilament Sewing Thread

I'm sure you've heard the stories, too. They usually go something like this:

"I was fishing at _____ Creek and was just tearing them up. I must have caught 50 fish, but no one else was catching anything. Want to know my secret? I use the monofilament sewing thread that you have to buy at the fabric store. It's the only way I caught those fish. The water was so clear, the trout were able to see everyone else's fishing line, but not mine!"

Sorry if this hurts your feelings, but this is another myth. In fact, it's one of the most widely held untruths regarding trout.

Fish story: Trout have amazing eyesight, so you have to use super-thin fishing line. Otherwise, they see the line and won't bite.

Before we jump into the meat of this topic, let's get the obvious out of the way. If a trout sees your line, they are not smart enough to recognize that it represents danger. To assume so is to anthropomorphize the fish. We humans obviously would recognize some string hanging from our cheeseburger and leading to the nearest lake, and we'd certainly hesitate before taking a bite, but that's our gray matter working. That said...

The reality is that a trout's eyesight is fine for what it needs to do, but our own eyesight is actually much better. In fact, while there is no way one can tell exactly what a trout sees, studying a trout's retina suggests that they're constructed pretty much like a human's. This would seem to indicate that a trout's eyesight is similar to what your eyesight is when you swim underwater with your eyes open — a bit fuzzy. Most people believe that fish have clear vision, similar to what you'd experience wearing goggles or a scuba mask, but that doesn't appear to be the case. There is no special covering to a trout's eye that accomplishes that effect. They do, however, have a lens that is spherical in shape. That helps them to focus in on items at different distances simultaneously, whereas our disk-shaped lens allows us to only focus on one plane of sight at a time. Even so, their best visual acuity is nowhere close to ours.

Think this through. If a trout spends his life eating tan colored mayfly nymphs, why in the world would he eat a lump of fur and feathers on a hook (better known as the Hare's Ear Nymph). Okay, it's about the right size, in the ballpark of the right shape, and about the right color. That's it. But, if you were to go swimming, opening your eyes underwater to watch a real nymph float by and then a Hare's Ear float by, guess what? They look very similar to each other when you "fuzz them out" a bit.

Then again, why should you believe me? What the heck do I know? Well, this is one area where I got obsessed with finding research that would prove or disprove my theory. I was initially able to "prove" it well enough for my own purposes, but only through anecdotal evidence, such as catching tons of "picky" trout on REALLY crummy flies using the line that was REALLY thick. But I needed scientific proof because this was one myth that just wouldn't go away without it. So, my apologies, but this is one of the rare times in this book that you'll have to endure something similar to real journalism.

As you probably know, the retina refers to the surface of the inside of the eye. Light enters the eye through the pupil, goes through the lens and hits the retina. If you were to look very very closely at the retina, you'd find little receptors called rods and cones. When the light hits the rods and cones, it transfers the raw data to the brain, and the brain makes the picture. We have WAY more rods and cones than trout do.

I remember visiting the Wild Animal Park on a trip to San Diego many years ago. At that time, they had a very cool bird show that I could talk about for hours. It was fantastic. But there was one thing in particular that really got my brain spinning. Without anyone noticing, a falcon left his cage backstage and climbed to a dizzying height, circling until called for. The bird trainer came out and started talking about how fast these birds were, throwing around some impressive numbers while putting on a big leather glove. He pointed skyward, the audience looked up and eventually found the tiny speck of the bird circling in his holding pattern. Then that bird dived straight down like he'd been shot out of a canon, came to a screeching halt and landed on the trainer's glove with zero impact. It was so sudden and so blindingly fast that everyone in the crowd let out a little "oh!" when it happened.

The trainer went on to explain that the bird's eyesight was thought to be about 10 times more acute than that of a human and that was one reason that the bird could zoom in so confidently. He also pointed to a tree on a hill above us that had a white square attached to it. At that distance, the white square looked about the size of a postage stamp, but the trainer explained that it was actually the size of a piece of notebook paper and had some well-known verse printed on it at the size of a normal typeface. The exact text escapes me now, but it was something famous like the preamble to the Constitution or maybe the Gettysburg Address. He described the bird's visual acuity by explaining that while humans couldn't even tell if there was text printed on that tiny white square, the bird perched on his hand could actually read it. I know what you're thinking. "They trained the bird to read?" I asked that same question. The laughter from the crowd really hurt my feelings.

I tell you that, so I can tell you this. The level of acuity in one's eyesight is directly related to how crowded the rods and cones are on the retina. So, assuming the trainer was correct about that bird's visual acuity, his rods and cones were crowded together 10x more densely than our own. Guess what? Our rods and cones are, in turn, crowded together 14 times more densely than a trout's. In other words, trout have more space between their rods and cones than we do — 14 times more space. So, if the difference between that falcon's eyesight and our eyesight is so dramatic, how much more dramatic is the difference between a trout's visual acuity and our own?

I can sense it! Crowds of readers, possibly including you, are now kind of squinting their eyes, pulling the corners of their lips up in a grimace and shaking their heads slowly. I know what that means. "Sorry, buddy, but I just don't buy it." That's okay. I totally understand how difficult it is to let go of something that seems so logical and embrace something else that seems to fly in the face of everything you know. Chill. I'm not done yet!

In the human eye, rods outnumber cones by about 17 to 1, which is by design. Rods specialize in seeing in low light conditions. Since there's less light, we need more rods to form the picture. Also, since there is less light, the image that the rods provide is mostly just black and white.

Cones, on the other hand, are very highly specialized. Humans have three different types of cones and each type receives data related to a specific primary color: red, yellow or blue. From those three colors, we can mix and match to form every color you've ever seen.

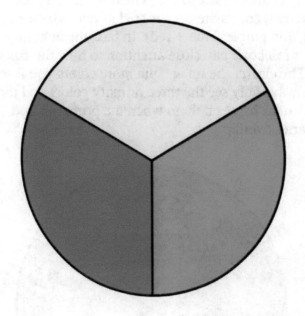

Primary Color Wheel

Interestingly, about 64% of our cones see red, 32% see yellow, and only 2% see blue. So, why do we see blue just as strongly as we see red? Because colors are filtered out of our vision by hazy conditions, low light levels, fog, rain, and even just air in the following order: red, yellow, blue. In other words, the first color we lose is red, then yellow, and then blue. Therefore, we have more "red" cones to compensate and we don't really need that many "blue" cones since it doesn't get filtered out until visibility is nearly zero. Neat, huh? Even so, red still disappears from our vision first, which is why a rose bush at twilight can appear to have green leaves and gray petals.

The primary visual color spectrum starts at red, gradually changes to yellow, then gradually changes to blue, and then gradually changes back to red. The transitional (aka "secondary") colors are orange (red + yellow), green (yellow + blue), and purple (blue + red). In fact, the next time you look at a rainbow, pay close attention to how the colors blend. The clearer the image, the more colors you'll see, but you'll always only see the three primary colors and the blended areas between them when the primaries and secondaries overlap.

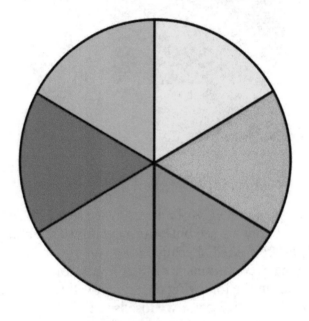

Primary and Secondary Color Wheel

Now you may be wondering why I say the visual color spectrum "starts" with red and "ends" with blue. It's because colors are actually defined by their wavelengths — shorter at one end of the spectrum and longer at the other — rather than by a wheel. It's not terribly important, really, but I like that the color wheel makes it easier for me to visualize the "invisible" colors with wavelengths too long or too short for our eyes to see. On the wheel, somewhere between red and purple is where you'll find ultraviolet (too short) and infrared (too long). This is one area where trout have us beat.

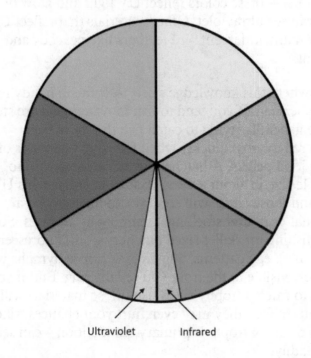

Ultraviolet   Infrared

Primary, Secondary, and Invisible Spectrum

Young trout have a fourth type of cone that can see ultraviolet. This specific cone is not active throughout a trout's life and they begin to shut down usually around his second birthday or shortly thereafter, but this ability is vital to the success of the species. So, why are trout born with this UV visibility skill?

A very large number of small aquatic insects have fluorescent qualities. Fluorescent simply means that they reflect ultraviolet light. So, since a newborn trout must eat massive amounts of food to fuel his growth over the first couple of years of his life, it is important for him to be able to key in on ultraviolet as a color. It is also for this reason that colors like chartreuse and fluorescent pink are so popular for fly and lure colors — these colors reflect UV light and glow brightly if you can see ultraviolet. Other materials that reflect UV include many iridescent bird feathers like peacock and pheasant.

Here's where this knowledge starts to come in handy for trout fishermen. If you tend to fish in waters that are stocked, you are generally trying to catch fish that have been engineered to grow quickly when fed large quantities of high-protein food pellets. A hatchery trout can be grown to stockable size in about a year. That trout still has his UV cones and those cones will continue to function for an additional year after stocking, assuming he survives. So, if you're fishing for skillet-sized hatchery trout, fluorescent flies like hot pink egg patterns, zug bugs or prince nymphs will be extremely visible to the trout you're targeting. But, if you're hoping to catch a trophy-sized fish, those materials will not help you. In fact, they may even hurt your chances, since smaller trout – a trophy's primary competition – can see it more readily.

Moreover, if you are fishing a river that includes wildly reproducing trout, using UV reflective materials in your baits and flies can lead to catching dozens of trout in the 8-inch and under category (0-2 years old). Since those trout are generally inexperienced and also tend to feed very competitively, the more mature trout may not have a chance to respond to your fly before those obnoxious little guys swarm on it.

I don't want to get too far down in the weeds here, so consider yourself lucky that I'm not going into iodopsins and response curves and such.

I'm betting this will be your first challenge question: "If a trout's eyesight is so darn crummy, how is it that they can track down a #24 midge emerger? If they're as borderline blind as you're suggesting, how is it that they can feed and survive at all?" Well, trout do certainly have some gifts. Their eyesight is based on movement — yes, just like the T-Rex in that dinosaur movie. In other words, even something small moving through their field of vision can be picked up visually. They are also quite gifted at seeing contrast, meaning they can easily see the color difference between your olive wooly bugger and the cloud of algae you just dragged it though. We know this due to the shape of their optic lens. Lastly, they also have the benefit of possessing a "tapetum lucidum," the thin retinal layer that makes your dog's eyes glow in the dark when the flashlight hits them just right. This reflective layer simply causes light that enters the eye to bounce around inside the eye. This magnifies the amount of light received by the rods in low-light conditions. In addition to these visual strengths, possibly their greatest advantage in the area of tracking prey is their unbelievably sensitive hearing.

There's been a significant quantity of debate over what exactly a fish's lateral line does, but biologists can at least agree that it picks up vibrations. Even more so, a good number of biologists believe this sense is so stunningly perceptive that they can use those vibrations to help them home in on their prey. In other words, they just might actually be able to "hear" that #24 midge emerger drifting toward them. We'll talk more about their sense of hearing a bit later.

And I'll bet this is challenge question #2: "If their eyesight is weak, then why do I see trout approach my fly, stare at it for a second, and turn away?" Well, not to put too fine a point on it, but trout have a provably and notably acute sense of smell. Touching your fly with their snout is not evidence of awesome vision. They're checking whether your fly smells like food. In fact, having to get that close to your fly is a better indicator that they can't see it very well.

So, once again, we have come full circle to address our original trout myth. No, they cannot see your line. However, since they can see movement and contrast so well, can you guess what they do see? Trout can easily see the shadow cast by your line on the water. How's that for a stunner? In fact, you can also see this shadow cast onto the creek bottom, if you look closely. What we're concerned about, though, is when that shadow lands on the fish. The shadow itself doesn't bother them – there are always leaves and twigs and whatnot floating by, after all — but the sudden movement of the shadow does upset them. And just like they'll bolt from your shadow or the shadow of a bird flying overhead, they'll bolt from the shadow your line is casting if it moves suddenly or unnaturally. And that actually DOES translate into a thinner fishing line offering a real benefit.

If you are a spin fisherman, ask yourself where, in relation to the fish, does your line enter the water. If you're simply casting and reeling an in-line spinner, you can use a very heavy line simply by keeping your rod tip DOWN, so the line enters the water at your feet. If you're rapidly twitching a jig, that entry point is going to be dancing all over the river, isn't it? In other words, it will be casting a rapidly twitching shadow down onto the fish. If that describes your fishing tactics, then you'll probably benefit from a thinner line, because a thinner line will cast a less noticeable shadow. If you are casting a dry fly, the thickness of the line MAY be an issue, but probably only if you like to twitch the fly. Again, the stationary shadow of the line floating on the water doesn't seem to bother the fish, but when that shadow moves, it's startling.

If you're drifting bait or a fly under a strike indicator or bobber, the MOST important thing related to line size is actually line flimsiness. A flimsy line will allow the fly or bait to tumble and drift naturally in the current, whereas a stiffer line will alter the drift. A trout will position himself in the current to intercept your bait or fly, but if the stiffer line alters its course, the trout will be out of position. It's that simple. In that case, line thickness is not the most important issue – stiffness vs. flimsiness is. So, a high-quality (flimsy) 6-pound test line will actually perform better than a poor quality (stiff) 4-pound test.

As I'm sure you can imagine, there are several other versions of trout mythos related to eyesight. And now that you have the background information, I'll bet you can answer any of the following assertions:

Fish story: Trout have such amazing eyesight, your flies and lures need to be exact duplicates.

Most of the little things that manufacturers add to their flies and lures are what could be called "fisherman catchers." If you use a fly or lure that's about the right size and shape, you'll catch plenty of fish. After all, what the heck does a wooly bugger look like? Just remember that everything looks fuzzy under water. Yes, trout can be selective, but that behavior is not related to their eyesight.

Fish story: Trout have such amazing eyesight, your dough bait or salmon egg must completely hide the point of the hook.

Their eyesight is simply not that good. However, if you're using a shiny gold hook and it's a bright sunshiny day, then it's possible that the hook will flash a bit in the sunshine. HOWEVER, since trout are stupid, this might actually HELP you catch fish. What's more likely, though, is that the trout's ultra-sensitive mouth feels the exposed hook when tasting it, causing him to expel it, which causes the bait to fall off the hook – aka "he stole my bait."

Fish story: Trout have such amazing eyesight, you have to trim the tag end of the line very close to the knot at the eye of the hook.

Yes, I know this is getting kind of silly, but this is another false belief that I've heard from time to time. Of course, the trout don't see the knot on your hook, but there are actually a few minor benefits to trimming the tag end of your knot. First, a long tag can catch debris and your fly, lure or bait will get soiled with algae and bits of leaves, etc. Second, it can actually change how your bait behaves. A long tag can cause a fly to lean this way or that instead of tumbling in a more random manner, for example. And third, since a trout's mouth is so sensitive, when they take the bait, there's a chance that they'll actually feel the too-long tag poking their mouth, causing them to spit it out more quickly.

Realistically, though, the above issues are not serious concerns. And since the trout cannot see the tag end of your knot, you don't need to trim it obscenely close. In fact, if you do, there's a chance that the tag will slip through the knot and the knot will untie itself while you're fighting that "fish of a lifetime." So, find a happy medium. Trim it a bit to help keep it clean, but don't go nuts with it.

Fish story: Trout have such amazing eyesight, you can catch more trout by using a fly with a bit of red tied in – it makes the fly look like it's bleeding.

This one is a mixed bag. Trout just don't have the brainpower to associate the color red with a bleeding injury, not to mention insects and crustaceans don't bleed. In fact, since red is filtered out of their vision first, it's probably not a color they use much to aid in feeding. Red might cause an "emotional" response of some sort if they get close enough to see it, but this is conjecture based on the knowledge that red is a spawning color in both rainbow and brown trout. But does it make your fly or lure actually work better? Beyond an individual fish's behavior, it's tough to tell.

In crystal clear water with the sun high in the sky, red appears completely gray at a fairly shallow depth, so adding red is likely counterproductive if your goal is to improve visibility. If that's what you're trying to accomplish, research shows that the color most visible to mature trout is essentially the same color that is most visible to us: bright yellow with just a touch of green, better known as "fire engine yellow." If you add some fluorescent quality to it, you'd call it "safety green." At any rate, on a bright sunny day, that is the color that trout will see the best.

However, if the lighting is subdued due to overcast conditions, or if you're fishing at night, most colors are less visible or completely invisible. In those circumstances, trout will key in on contrast, meaning black and white are often the best options. White reflects visible light best, so it often is the most visible color during overcast conditions when other colors begin to appear gray. Black is always the most visible color at night, because it absorbs the ambient light better, creating a solid high-contrast silhouette.

As a final thought, keeping in mind that the colors with the longest wavelengths (reds) are filtered out of visibility first, it makes sense that the colors with shortest wavelengths remain visible from a greater distance. Therefore, it also makes sense that the visible color with the shortest wavelength (violet) is filtered out last. That knowledge can come in handy when you're fishing a more sparsely populated trout stream, requiring you to draw fish from a greater distance to come look at your fly.

HOWEVER, if you're getting skunked and you just want to catch some trout regardless of size, that's a great time to break out the fluorescent colors, because they shine brightly in the UV light that is present even under thick gray clouds. As previously discussed, it won't help you attract those lunkers, but at least you'll catch some fish.

Visibility doesn't always lead to bites, of course. Sometimes something different is needed to trigger the take and red is a potential candidate. I've tested this over the years by adding red to traditional flies and switching back and forth between the two matching patterns — "regular" pheasant tail vs. "bit" pheasant tail, for example. The results have not been earth-shattering, but I must admit, I'm leaning toward the conclusion that a little red just might be enough to get that curious fish to bite once they've gotten close enough to inspect the fly. More research is called for here (dag nabbit), but this may be one of those myths that are not exactly true but still might help you catch a few more fish regardless.

Obviously, the real trick is to balance all of this information into a single fly or tandem rig. Maybe a fly with fire engine yellow to catch their attention, purple or blue to enhance long-distance visibility, and red to trigger the bite when the trout comes within striking distance? If anyone wants to invent that fly, mail me a few. I'll start testing them immediately.

CHAPTER SIX

Give Me A Ping Vasili.
One Ping Only Please.

If you get that reference, 10 points to Gryffindor. And if you have any childhood memories of fishing with grandpa, then you probably recall being shushed to avoid scaring the fish. Guess what?

Fish story: No talking while fishing! The fish can hear you talking and they will not bite!

Trout actually DO have an amazing sense of hearing, BUT no, they cannot hear you talking. The good news is that trout only hear what vibrates through the water, so your voice is pretty much a non-issue. Trout can hear sounds that vibrate the earth, like large tree branches falling, nearby traffic sounds, gunshots, thunder, etc., as those vibrations move from the earth and air into the water, but the normal above water sounds that you and your fishing buddy might produce? Nope, not a problem. The bad news is that their sensitivity to subsurface sounds is astounding and we trout fishermen need to tread lightly!

Fish don't have ears in the traditional land animal sense. They are instead equipped to take full advantage of water as a medium for vibrations, and that specialized equipment is the lateral line. The lateral line runs down the length of the fish's body and is comprised of specialized receptor cells called neuromasts. I don't want to geek out on you too much, so we can leave the scientific description there. But, it is important to understand that a fish's sense of hearing is more than what we experience. They likely comprehend sounds in the traditional sense, as we do, but they also comprehend actual physical vibration caused by disruptions in the water — a kind of "distant touch."

Have you ever been outside when lightning strikes nearby? The almost instantaneous blast of thunder probably caused a shock wave that you literally felt hitting your body. Or maybe you experienced this at the last big fireworks display you watched. That shock wave was heard, of course, but even if you were completely deaf, you still would have felt it. And even without seeing the flash, you still would have reacted by looking in the right direction. As I write this, I live near an educational mine managed by Missouri University of Science and Technology (Go Miners!). I'm still always stunned when they set off explosives. Not only do I hear the sound, I can actually feel the thud. As further evidence, I can also hear the windows and doors of my house vibrate with the blast, starting at one corner of my house and zipping toward the opposite end.

Now, what if you had neuromasts along the length of your body that funneled those vibrations directly into your brain? Yikes! Do you think that shock wave startled you before? With your new lateral line, you'd have a heart attack (or at least wet your pants)! But imagine how much detail you could absorb from more normal sounds like footsteps on dry leaves. You'd grasp the size of the sound, the location, and the direction of movement. If someone threw a rock at you, you might even sense it coming and know to duck out of the way without having to rely on your eyesight. Humans already have some limited echo-location ability. You can test your own ability by turning on some quiet background noise (like a fan), closing your eyes and slowly bringing your hands to your ears without touching them. Oddly, it doesn't work as well in a loud environment. Give it a try. Nifty, eh?

If you've ever had the opportunity to watch a school of fish swarm this way and that, you've probably been blown away by their ability to avoid running into each other. And since their eyesight isn't as great as some would have you believe, it's almost as if they have a sixth sense, right? Well, they kinda do! Their sense of hearing really is more like sonar, telling them what's going on in the water around them — even from a great distance. Bass fishermen figured this out years ago and promptly started adding rattlers to their crankbaits and rubber worms to help the bass home in on the lure. Trout fishermen have not learned how to really take advantage of this ability, however. That is largely due to the fact that normal-sized trout are not typically aggressive ambush feeders, so odd sounds (like a rattler in a crankbait) would tend to make them nervous rather than triggering a "can I eat it?" response. BUT, understanding how a trout hears can and should affect how you go after them.

Picture an enormous fish tank about one foot deep, approximately the size of a football field, with a trout hanging out at one corner of the tank. If you could eliminate all residual vibration in the water (i.e. absolute silence), that trout would clearly "hear" the sound of a marble dropped into the tank at the corner opposite from him. But, in addition to hearing it, he would also grasp the size and the location of the item. How do we know this? Because fisheries graduate students get to do all kinds of fun and interesting experiments like this, just so their thesis will be accepted and their advanced degree awarded. And a quick internet search will find stacks and stacks of fascinating (albeit dry) reading on topics such as this.

In the above example, the students hypothesized that brown trout could recognize the sizes and locations of pellets dropped into the water at a distance. They tested this (and many would say proved it) by dropping food pellets, as well as non-food pellets, of various other sizes into the water. Once the trout identified which size of "plop" was the correct size for food, the students were able to document reactions to the sounds accordingly. For example, the fish would physically react to a non-food pellet, but would not bother to approach it to investigate. A food pellet, on the other hand, made the "correct" sound when dropped in and was quickly pursued and eaten.

This power is one of the trout's greatest weapons as well as a fantastic defense mechanism. As a weapon, the trout uses this ability to aid in feeding. So, if you've ever wondered how a trout can successfully feed on nearly invisible midge emergers, it may be that they can actually feel those tiny bugs drifting toward them or swimming to the surface, even making it possible to nibble on drifting tidbits in the dark. And as a defense mechanism, any sudden unexpected vibration in the water sends those fish into a real tizzy. An otter swishing around in the river or the splash of an osprey or bear are not recognized as the sounds of specific threats, but they are startling and outside of the norm. In the same fashion, when a tree limb breaks free and hits the water, the trout scatter for cover. And when you rip your fly line off the surface or stumble over a rock while wading, guess what? Those startling sounds are costing you fish – a whole lot of fish. There is good news, though: trout are stupid!

When I was about 11 years old, I had a "special fishing buddy" for a short time. I put that in quotes because this guy was a real "treat" to fish with. I put "treat" in quotes because I don't really mean it. See the trend here? It only took me one full summer to finally cut him loose, but what a wild summer! I wandered away from my stringer of rock bass one day and when I got back the fish were gone. He'd tossed them back in "for me" because they had all died and were no longer "fit to eat." Notice all the quotes? When I tell stories about this kid to current-day friends, my quote-drawing fingers spend a lot of time in the air. Another time, I caught a bass that measured 12 inches, which was a legal size for the creek we were fishing. He argued with me about the measurement, telling me it was only 11-1/2 inches and that he'd turn me in as a poacher if I kept it. A couple of weeks later, he kept several sub-legal bass. When I challenged him on his hypocrisy, he said: "I ain't afraid of no game warden." Nice, huh?

He had one trick he liked to pull that still makes me shake my head when I think about it. I was fishing a good-looking spot on the Roubidoux Creek near Waynesville, Missouri, and I was having a bit of luck. After stringing up my second trout, he stopped fishing, put down his rod and started wandering the bank behind me like he was looking for something. Turns out, he was looking for just the right grapefruit-sized rock. You guessed it. An enormous SPLASH right in the middle of my fishing spot scared me out of my shoes. His explanation? He was "helping," of course! Throwing a big rock in your spot was meant to "wake up the fish," so you'd catch more! The first time he pulled that, I yelled and screamed and threatened, but ultimately decided that maybe he was just an idiot and really thought it was true. But when he did it a second time a few weeks later, I knew it was time we parted ways.

I'm certainly not encouraging you to start chucking rocks into your favorite fishing spot, but I did discover something that summer. After he tried to spoil my fishing the first time, and after I threw my temper tantrum, he left. I nearly left too, but there was enough doubt about whether he believed his own BS, that I had to give it a shot. And about 15 minutes or so after the big rock hit the water, I was once again catching trout in that spot. I had a bit of guilt for yelling at him, I must admit. Could it be that throwing a big rock in the creek could actually "wake them up?" The short answer is, yes, it can startle them into a more alert state, but that certainly doesn't make them bite. What I had witnessed that day was simply evidence that fish have a short attention span.

Years later, I developed an interest in observing trout behaviors up close and started spending a good amount of time watching without fishing. Sitting on a high bank on a sunny day, I was able to watch fish actively feeding. And then, for fun, I tossed in one of those grapefruit-sized rocks. The fish completely freaked out, of course. But 10 minutes later, those fish were right back in their favorite feeding lanes, leisurely feeding on drifting bugs as if nothing had happened. When I tossed in another rock, I saw the same behaviors. It was fascinating.

That story is a long way to go for what I'm about to tell you, but here it is. I've fished with a great many fishermen over the years and a good percentage of them just don't know how to keep the water quiet. They routinely stumble while wading or simply wade far too quickly, leaving a splash wake behind them. They rip the water with their fly line, they slap the water with their flies or plunk their styrofoam strike indicator. But even if you're guilty of these offenses, hope is not lost.

 While trout can't hear sounds that are passing above the surface of the water, those subsurface sounds made by crunching gravel, kicking over rocks, stepping on twigs, etc. are certainly experienced by every fish in the river. But, since they're not very smart, they really just need a few minutes to calm down. After all, it might have just been a tree limb hitting the water, right? Not a bear. Not an osprey. Not a fisherman. Just a tree limb.

So, the best advice I can offer is this. Stay out of the water, if you can. If you have to wade, move slowly and as quietly as possible. And work on your casting and mending, to make the process as delicate and quiet as possible. Don't cast downward toward the water. Cast above the water, parallel to the surface, so the line straightens and your fly, lure or bait will drop to the water with the force of only gravity. We all struggle to stay within those parameters at times, of course, but understanding your objective is the first step to reaching it.

If you're fishing a wild little trout creek that receives almost no fishing pressure, silence is golden and often an absolute necessity. If you're fishing a river with more activity – a lot of fishermen shuffling around, canoes scraping through riffles, kids and dogs swimming, etc. – the trout quickly become accustomed to a certain level of disturbance and they are generally more forgiving of a stumble in the rocks or a ripped cast. And if you screw up, take a break and let the fish calm down. Of course, there are disturbances that can put fish off their feed for hours (I'm looking at you jet boaters), but for the most part, a little noise isn't going to ruin your day.

CHAPTER SEVEN

Sooner Or Later, Every Trout Will Eat A Yellow Glo-bug

I've tried very hard to study and learn about what a trout eats, but it's SOOOOO boring (hint: it's usually bugs). For that reason, I opted to focus on how a trout CHOOSES what to eat. That's actually a fairly simple thing, but it will fly in the face of a number of trout myths. I've heard these beliefs voiced in a wide variety of ways, but they can generally be condensed into the following:

Fish story: Only freshly-stocked hatchery trout will take a glo-bug or a salmon egg. Wild and resident trout are too smart for baits like that.

I'm not psychic, but I'd be willing to bet some of you are responding to the above with a thought something like "this is kinda true, though, isn't it?" Well, like most things, the best answer is "it depends."

As I've said before, I'm a firm believer that most things you'll find attached to your fly shop trout fly (i.e. legs, wing cases, antennae, etc.) are actually there to catch the fisherman. I developed that belief on a summertime Colorado fishing trip, during which I was planning to spend a few days of my vacation hitting the Colorado River between Hot Sulphur Springs and Parshall, with a special focus on Byer's Canyon. I already knew that a primary food source for those trout were great big brown-to-black stoneflies. So, in preparation for my trip, I tied a couple of dozen flies to match – more than enough! Right? Well…

The fishing was far better than I'd expected. It was so fantastic, in fact, that I ended up spending the better part of a week fishing close to 5 miles of river and my supply of stoneflies was going fast. By the end of day 5, the fishing had suddenly slowed down, which was fine. I only had a couple of flies left and they were looking pretty rough. To both celebrate a great 5 days on the river and simultaneously mourn the last day on the river, I must admit to spending too much time with Mr. Beam that evening and therefore opted to sleep in a tad the following morning while my blood detoxified.

When I finally dragged my sorry tail out of the tent, I decided to spend one last day on the river before breaking camp. This was a Saturday, so there were a few other fishermen out and about. When I crossed paths with one of them heading home, I asked for a report and was told, "They're pretty tough today. Nothing like the last couple of weeks." It was the report I was dreading, but I soldiered on regardless. After all, I already had my waders on. And I have to say, that fisherman was right. They were tough that Saturday. And yet, I still caught fish on those beat up raggedy leftover flies. In fact, the final two hookups of the day came on my last stonefly that was essentially nothing more than brown dubbing wrapped the length of the hook. No more shell casing. No more hackle. No more antennae. And as I headed back to camp, I had the opportunity to talk to two more fishermen to compare notes. At the risk of sounding big-headed, I had out-fished them both with my ratty stonefly-colored fur bugs.

So, what did I deduct from that experience? Well, if I had caught 50 fish on day 6, I would have chalked my success up to stupid fish. After all, I had caught ridiculous numbers of fish on days 1 through 5, so they were obviously feeding aggressively. I would have assumed that IN THIS SPECIFIC SITUATION the fish were stupid enough that I might have caught them on a bare hook, but that's not the hypothesis I developed. Instead, because the fishing was tough, I began wondering if my belief that flies had to include little details like antennae and legs to fool the smarter fish was – not to put too fine a point on it – a load of crap. Out came my scientist's hat and I determined to test this hypothesis wholeheartedly. I'm sure you know what I discovered.

My subsequent testing over the next several months included switching between traditional pheasant tail nymphs and bare bones pheasant tails tied only with wrapped pheasant and peacock, comparing tightly tied elk hair caddis to big yellow humpies, offering realistically tied baitfish streamers and the good old wooly bugger, plopping Dave's Hoppers in the summertime interspersed with plopping muddler minnows like a hopper, and even switching between stoneflies and wooly worms tied in a similar size and color. And 90% of the time, I found no notable difference in results. The only time that the trout routinely turned their nose up at the "ugly" fly was during a hatch. At those times, it was important to offer at least a decent match for the nymph, emerger, adult, spinner, or spent-wing that the trout were keying in on. In your area, you may discover that a "hatch" also includes non-bug food items. For example, egg flies fished during a spawn, white leech patterns fished in tailwaters after a shad kill, exact scud patterns when scuds are migrating, etc. Regardless, the principle is still sound. Aside from those instances, however, the fly did not appear to be the most important piece of the puzzle. In fact, sometimes a fly that's a bit too big or too brightly colored would actually work better than a "perfect" match. After all, their eyesight isn't that great, right?

My quasi-scientific study in this regard led me to some answers, of course, but even more valuable, it led to new questions that I was then obsessed to answer. And by continuing to game-plan my fishing trips and my tactics, I've come to believe that trout feed in one of four primary ways: aggressively, opportunistically, naturally, and selectively.

Aggressive Feeding

I'm sure you've experienced it before. No matter what bait you cast, it seems like every trout in the river freaks out and races to snatch it, nearly pulling your rod arm out of socket. Those are special moments and they are loads of fun – although it doesn't do much for your self-esteem since every hack on the water is hooking fish. But what causes it?

First of all, the fish have to actually be hungry, of course. And since all fish are cold-blooded, their metabolism is directly related to the water temperature, meaning the warmer the water, the hungrier the fish. Second, the fish have to be enjoying a high-oxygen environment. If you and I ran a foot race on Pike's Peak, I'd probably pass out before I hit 100 yards, simply because there's not enough oxygen to move my impressive girth.

Physical performance all starts with oxygen. When you become physically active, your body aerobically (aka "with oxygen") converts stored glycogen into glucose to burn as energy — no oxygen, no glucose. Once the glucose is burned, your body consumes increasing quantities of oxygen in an effort to replenish your glucose supply. If this continues, you'll eventually move into the anaerobic (aka "without oxygen") category of physical exertion, when you begin burning acids as fuel — lactic, amino, and fatty. This means you're not consuming enough oxygen to keep up with your glucose requirements. If you're a trout, anaerobic physical exertion means you're in trouble.

After anaerobic activity has concluded, oxygen consumption is required to burn off or flush out the acids that have collected in the muscle tissues. This recovery is vital to a fish's survival. It's also the reason we C&R fishermen take our time reviving trout by holding them in the current until they've recovered enough to swim away.

The bottom line is this: the more oxygen you have available to you for consumption, the greater the physical endurance you will enjoy. There's a reason athletes have been known to suck on O2 tanks on the sidelines. As we've already covered in chapter 4, the colder the water, the more dissolved oxygen it can hold. Rainfall, white-capped riffles and waterfalls all oxygenate the water quickly, but even a still water pond will gradually absorb oxygen from the atmosphere until it reaches its carrying capacity. And as the water warms, it sheds dissolved oxygen.

If you can balance those two conditions – warm enough to be hungry, but cold enough to be high oxygen – you'll usually find active fish. For rainbow and brown trout in my part of the country, finding those peak conditions generally means a fairly consistent water temperature of around 60 degrees.

There's something else to bear in mind. Of course, there is. We wouldn't want things to be too simple, right? My local waters are spring-fed streams or big tailwaters, and both types of rivers have very consistent temperatures at their sources. Most of our springs start out at 53 or 54 degrees, while the temperatures of tailwaters vary depending on how deep the lake is on the other side of the dam. Tailwaters can be VERY cold at their source, but they can also suffer from VERY low dissolved oxygen levels at certain times of the year since the waters are being siphoned from a lake often several hundred feet deep. It should also be noted that groundwater is often low in oxygen, depending on how deep the spring pool is and whether it flows through an oxygenated cave system or not. In other words, the cold headwaters of your favorite trout streams are not necessarily where you'll find the best action. If you live in an area where most trout waters are fed by runoff or snow-melt, you shouldn't find this to be a problem.

In addition to finding the water conditions that are in that sweet spot — cold enough for oxygen, warm enough for hunger — there's a third variable. Without going into too much detail at this point (we'll cover it later, I promise), there are two primary spawning seasons for fish: spring and fall. Certain strains of trout have been known to spawn over the winter months, but we'll keep things simple for now. As the spawning season for a specific fish approaches, those fish get very excited. They move upstream, they begin to crowd into smaller habitat, and they begin to feel very competitive with each other. And, when hormones are floating around in the water, the males of that species get STUPID and the rest of the fish in the river, regardless of species, perk up as well. If you can time your trip to coincide with hunger, oxygen, and hormones, you're going to have a great time. But even if the water temperatures aren't cooperating, the hormones are often enough to get those fish acting crazy. At those times, just tie on an obvious fly, and hang on. That type of behavior is what I call "Aggressive Feeding." Pretty creative, huh?

Opportunistic Feeding

While an aggressively feeding trout is one that will chase a 5-inch streamer halfway to grandma's house, a fish that is feeding opportunistically is just a bit more relaxed about life. Trout are, by nature, opportunistic feeders. This means that if you were to stumble upon a wild population of trout that have never been fished before, you'd probably tear them up with any edible-looking fly in your box. For that matter, you can catch plenty of opportunistically feeding fish on anything (yes, anything) that looks like it might be tasty.

During my trout observations, I am frequently able to watch trout leisurely tasting anything that drifts by – sticks, leaves, cottonwood fluff, etc. In the mouth it goes and out it pops, as soon as they realize it's not edible. On one such excursion, I watched a small rainbow suspiciously approach a great big beetle that had been blown onto the river. That beetle went into and out of that trout's mouth 4 or 5 times before the trout finally decided it was something good enough to eat. It seemed to me that he'd never eaten a beetle before, but I'll bet he kept his eye open for more of them in the future.

One of my favorite places to observe trout is several hundred yards downstream from a highly pressured bait fishing area. While observing those fish, the occasional bit of floating dough bait will drift by and those opportunistically feeding trout will take it in, spit it out, sniff it, take it again, and so on until they decide it's edible. This behavior really makes perfect sense when you think about it. After all, how does a newborn trout learn to eat a bug? Sooner or later, he has to taste something. If it's soft and squishy and tastes good, they eat it. Otherwise, they spit it right back out.

It's for this reason that every trout in the river will eventually get hooked on something. Even if you're fishing with a bait they've never seen before, there will come a time when they're relaxed and hungry and curious, and everything will be tasted. If you're quick enough to set the hook, you're golden.

In 1988, the world record brown trout at that time was caught in Arkansas on a treble hook with a kernel of corn on each point, and a mini-marshmallow on the shank. The fish weighed nearly 39 pounds, once again proving that even great big trout, at least occasionally, make stupid decisions.

Natural Feeding

When trout are feeding more naturally, they are often also feeding somewhat passively and you might perceive them as not being very hungry. A naturally feeding trout will still eat bits of food that drift by, but he's just not all that interested in expanding his horizons at that moment in time. This doesn't necessarily mean he's not hungry. It might mean he's distracted, nervous, or struggling with low oxygen content during the warmer months. But, of course, lack of hunger may also be the case. It could be that the water is so cold that his metabolism and need for calories are extremely low. Or maybe you got there right after a major hatch and his tummy is just stuffed full of bugs after a terrific feeding frenzy. And you already know there's nothing worse than hearing, "you shoulda been here a couple of hours ago!" Natural feeding is not the end of the world, though. You just have to take your job a bit more seriously.

A naturally feeding trout will find a lie where he feels comfortable and is not burning a lot of energy. If this includes a good supply of food, it's a bonus, but feeding may not be his primary concern. This is a comfort zone thing. First and foremost, he's looking for a position where he feels safe and calm. In other words, you may have to cover more water and cast to spots you might normally ignore, fishing typical feeding areas as well as some slower uglier water. While a more actively feeding trout will likely stay close to feeding lanes, passively feeding trout can be scattered all over the place.

When trout are feeding naturally, the larger percentage of your hook-ups will come on flies and baits that look familiar to the fish or look similar to the bugs that are most active at the time. But the primary issue for a fisherman trying to catch a passively feeding trout is that his strike zone is simply smaller. In fact, this style of feeding represents the smallest strike zone you're likely to see when trout fishing.

To be clear, "strike zone" refers to the distance a trout is willing to move to intercept potential food. So when the strike zone is small (i.e. 6 inches), you either need to drift your fly right to the trout's nose, or you need to offer something that is so tempting that it might increase the strike zone a bit and trigger a more emotional "oh boy!" reaction. By comparison, when trout are feeding aggressively and the strike zone is at its largest, all you need to do is offer something that looks interesting and they'll chase your bait across the river to grab it.

Catching a passively feeding trout can be challenging, but you already know that. It's the nature of the challenge that can be confusing. When you arrive at the river and a departing fisherman tells you the fishing has been tough or the bite has been slow, THIS is probably what's happening. Tie your boot laces snugly, eat a protein bar, and plan to cover some territory.

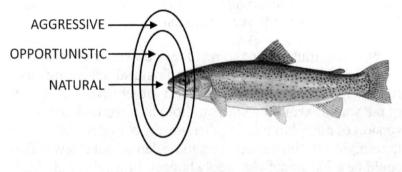

The Strike Zone

If a trout's strike zone has shrunk due to feeling nervous or distracted (i.e. swimmers nearby, a sudden flood of fishermen, a sudden crowd of canoeists, a jet boat zipping by recently, etc.), you can still catch that fish by drifting natural-looking bits of food right to his snout. But, to be honest, making that cast without chasing away this nervous fish is tough, which is why I will often move away toward a less distracting environment to find fish who are more relaxed. Conversely, however, if the noise and commotion have been going on for some time, the trout can actually become accustomed or desensitized to it and you can catch fish right in the midst of the craziness. You can pull fish out between canoes filled with noisy river rats or 30 feet upstream of a group of swimming kids. It may seem strange, but if the background noise is consistent, they apparently stop considering it to be threatening and go on about their business.

If the trout are legitimately not hungry, then you're likely fishing during an excessively cold time of the year, or your timing is just crummy – showing up immediately after a major hatch, for example. These fish are also still catchable. Think back to Thanksgiving. Even though your pants were bursting at the seams, you still managed to choke down that piece of pumpkin pie, right? Of course, you're going to eat it! It just looks too good! Same principle.

Now, since trout are not going to turn down a free meal, you can catch this fish by drifting a bit of natural-appearing food right to his snout – they'll often eat it rather than moving out of the way to avoid it – but you shouldn't overlook the trout version of pumpkin pie. In other words, consider a bait or fly that might get him excited on a more "emotional" level. This could be a big stonefly, a wooly bugger, or a yellow glo-bug. There's no rhyme or reason as to what gets that specific trout excited enough to expand his strike zone and move farther to take this bait rather than that one, so I generally just choose something that's obvious and visible.

But what about those full-tummy trout that won't be swayed by your obvious bait? Those are the fish that will legitimately only eat a small natural food item that drifts right to him. But I promise you this: he noticed that glo-bug. And that gives you an advantage if you're willing and able to fish a two-fly rig.

By fishing a lead fly that is meant as an attention-getter and trailing a small natural-looking fly 18 inches behind, you can get the best of both of those fish. The "oh boy" fly (i.e. a yellow glo-bug) will draw every trout's gaze and prompt a few of them to widen their strike zone to take the fly. But even if they don't take, they'll at least be looking in the right direction just in time to see that small natural-looking tidbit of food drifting right behind. And seeing two bits of potential food (rather than just one) following the same path can be the tipping point to get trout to move, enlarging the strike zone. So, simply adding that small nymph or scud can be killer in this situation. But, then, "killer" is a relative term, isn't it?

You'll still be covering a lot of water, casting and drifting through ugly spots as well as those traditionally fishy-looking locations, making a lot more casts than normal in the effort to get that fly to drift into or at least nearby a tiny strike zone. But the good news is that a fish that's not hungry is also not territorial. That means that once you find a fish, you'll probably find several because when they're not feeling territorial, trout will school up. So, once you get a hit, STOP and fish that spot hard. You may be glad you did.

That said, there is another circumstance when trout are feeding passively. The good news is, in this last circumstance, they are HUNGRY.

Every fishing season begins with springtime aggressive feeding, but as summer gets here and progresses into seriously hot days, the fishing tends to get tough. A predictable pattern, right? But why does the bite seem to slow down? There are a few reasons, actually. First, the water is usually lower and clearer, making the fish feel less safe. Second, the aquatic insect activity tends to drop, since most hatch activity happens in the spring and fall. A lot of drifting food decreases the fear associated with feeding. But in areas where trout streams tend to warm up in the summer, it's that pesky dissolved oxygen again. The warmer the water, the lower the oxygen, meaning Mr. Trout's physical endurance is at a low point. And that, of course, simply means he's not physically capable of pursuing food.

But there is a reason that hot-weather passive feeding is different from the other types of passive feeding, and that is hunger. In warm water, the cold-blooded trout experience an elevated metabolism. In fact, he's burning calories like they're going out of style and he desperately needs as many calories as he can get... as long as he can do it without breathing heavy. And that is why you need to bring that $50 filet mignon to that fish and put it on his TV tray. That means BIG flies.

Do a bug sampling and identify the largest insect present and offer a reasonable imitation a size or two too big. Or tie on a big heavy streamer and twitch it slowly on the bottom from an upstream position. If you twitch near a trout's nose, he's going to grab it. For that matter, even that big yellow glo-bug can be a winner, since the fish are desperate for calories. Anything that looks like a potential meal will be accepted if you can get it close enough to him.

As for fishing spots, you can probably skip the ugly water this time. Since they're hungry and out of breath, they'll set up in spots that require very little energy expenditure with easy access to a faster current that will bring drifting food. This is where you would normally look for feeding fish, but the difference is their tiny strike zone. They're just not going to move much unless you're offering something that looks to be full of calories.

HOWEVER, keep this in mind. When the dissolved oxygen content is low and a trout's metabolism is up, the mortality rate of trout caught and released is inevitably higher than normal. By playing a fish to exhaustion, you've allowed him to build up a potentially toxic level of metabolic acids. And with a low level of oxygen, it will take quite some time for him to recover. Therefore, I hope you'll choose one of the two following suggestions: (1) don't fish during the dog days of summer – just leave the fish alone; or (2) if you do fish during those super hot weeks, land your fish quickly and plan to take as long as it takes to fully revive him in the current prior to releasing him. The trout gods will reward you!

Selective Feeding

Since we've already spent some time on the subject of selective feeding, I'll just revisit it briefly rather than bore you with redundancies. It is notable, however, that this fourth style of feeding is not related to the feeding strike zone discussed earlier in this chapter. When trout are feeding selectively, it is the only time when your fly selection becomes the most critical part of your formula for success. It also means that your success has very little to do with the trouts' metabolism, the quantity of dissolved oxygen in the water, spawning season hormones, or even attitude. It's almost all about the bugs.

Previously, I compared selective feeding to a teenager blindly working his way through a bag of potato chips. If we want to look at it more realistically, you have to "be the trout." Put yourself in the trout's mind and imagine looking directly into the current as bugs and debris drift past you on all sides (mostly debris). In addition to edibles, there are bits of leaves, specks of dust, seeds, algae, and other aquatic plant matter, sticks, and so on, all drifting right at you and all around you. Your job is to pick through the cloud of garbage to find the bits of food. During a hatch, instead of 10% of the specks being food, 90% of the specks may be food, and they all look about the same. As a trout, all the non-edible specks in the water become nothing more than background noise to you at a time like this. They're not looking at your fly and refusing it. It's just part of the static. Can you see it?

This is another circumstance where fishing tandem rigs can be very beneficial, but properly fishing a hatch with a tandem rig is more complex than just tying on a dry fly and dragging a nymph underneath it. Instead, consult your inside information sources regarding local hatches to help you use the rig to stay ahead of the hatch.

Most fishermen have never thought through how a trout works a hatch. Instead, when we hear those magic words — "the Green Drakes are up!" or something similar — we charge down to the river and start throwing dry flies. If this sounds like you, you're missing out.

We covered this in chapter 3, but it's important enough to revisit it briefly. A few hours before you see bugs in the air, the nymphs are starting to get active. Depending on the species, they'll start off by kicking up into the current and drifting downstream, swimming back down to the gravel. The next step may include swimming to the surface, back down to the gravel, and then back to the surface like a yo-yo. Eventually, they'll start their emergence, drifting in the surface film, cracking open up their shell, and fighting their way out. Once they're free, they'll ride the surface until their wings dry enough to become flight worthy. Then they're off! Meanwhile, some of the bugs that hatched a day or two prior are returning to mate and lay eggs on the water, making them accessible to the trout a second time. It's important to understand this process because this is how the trout see the hatch.

On one of my local rivers, there's a big hatch that many of the locals refer to as a "white fly" hatch. That's not actually the correct name for the bug, as a whitefly looks like a little white housefly while these specific bugs are among a few different species of light-colored mayflies that share the same nickname. Regardless, my local whitefly nymphs are silt burrowing, meaning the trout are generally not aware of them at all and the entire hatch from start to finish is usually over in just a couple of hours. They dig out and make it to the surface before they hit the first set of riffles downstream from their home. Occasionally, you'll see trout taking the adults off the surface, but the more common observation will be tens of thousands of bugs in the air and not a ring to be seen. That's because trout work a hatch from the gravel up, taking nymphs first, following them as they swim to the surface and wriggle in the surface film, eventually taking the adults. If you want to catch those trout, start deep.

There's a creek not far from my home that has a great Blue Wing Olive population. During hatch season, my fly box typically includes a straight-shank traditional "drifter" nymph, a bent-shank "swimmer" nymph, an emerger, a parachute dry, a dun version, a spinner version, and a spent wing. Upon arriving at the creek, I first stop to look for apparent feeding behaviors. Are there bugs in the air? Are the fish dimpling or tailing? Those are tell-tale signs of where to start. But, if there's nothing obvious going on, I'll start with the swimmer nymph as my lead fly and the drifter nymph as my trailer. I want the two flies to drift at different depths in this case, so I'll only weight the trailer.

Assuming I catch some fish, the trout will tell me where they are in the hatch cycle simply by preferring one fly over the other. If I'm catching trout on the bottom fly, then I picked right. If I'm catching fish mostly on my top fly, I'll change my rig, because the trout are telling me that they've already begun to follow the hatch higher into the water column.

My new lead fly will be the emerger and the swimming nymph will be demoted to the trailer. Eventually, as the hatch progresses, the trout will stop taking the swimmer and move up to the emerger, triggering me to change my rig again. Time to fish a parachute with an emerger trailing behind. And so on, and so on. When I time it right, I can fish that hatch for hours and catch a ridiculous quantity of fish, including some very nice-sized fully mature whoppers.

Keep in mind, selective feeding means the trout are feeding without fear. They're so focused on the food, they don't have any extra attention to spare for things like predators or fishermen. So, if you pick the right fly at the right time, you'll find them hungry and fearless. What's not to like about that?

CHAPTER EIGHT

Spooky Trout Grow Up

It's always fun to stumble upon a trout stream where the fish seem to have no fear, allowing you to stomp over to them, kicking over rocks along the way, slapping your line on the water, and still managing to catch as many fish as you want. It's always a great day, but there's a big downside. Those rivers usually don't have very many trophy-sized fish.

Fish story: Trophy-sized trout are extra-smart. That's how they've avoided being caught for all those years. So, only the best fishermen catch lunkers, unless they get very, very lucky.

I certainly don't want to make anyone feel bad about themselves, but if you've ever had the pleasure of catching a trophy trout – or a trophy fish of any kind, for that matter – chances are you were simply extremely lucky. Trophy trout are definitely different than more typically-sized fish, but the differences are not what most people expect.

Before we go much further, though, let's be clear about something. We are likely talking about different things when we discuss trophy fish. Most people have a specific size in mind when they think "trophy," but that size is based on the rivers they consider to be their home waters. That means your definition of "trophy" is likely different from mine.

As a fly-fishing guide, I take clients to three very different destinations. On the largest of the three rivers, the average-sized fish we catch is probably 13 inches or so, with 10% of the fish in the 18-inch category. Each year, we hook at least a couple of fish in the 22- to 24-inch long ballpark. And based on those results, 20 inches seems to be the lower end of the size for a fish to be considered "mountable," and 24 inches is considered a "real monster." Most of our spring-fed rivers can't support trout a whole lot bigger than that, although bigger ones are out there in very small numbers.

If you hop in the truck and head south a couple hundred miles, you'll find yourself in Arkansas tailwater country. If you've done any reading in trout fishing magazines, and I'm betting you have, you've probably heard of the White, the Norfork, and the Little Red, all part of the same system of tailwaters, cold water rivers pulled from the bottom of deep-water dams. Tailwaters usually boast a ridiculously abundant food supply of scud, sowbugs, midges, and various other little critters, as well as baitfish, suckers, and sculpins. And being big water with consistent temperatures and a fantastic food supply, these rivers grow enormous fish – although they may grow fairly slowly due to the colder water temperatures suppressing their metabolism at times.

If you were to take a week-long fishing trip and hit those rivers, you'd almost be guaranteed to hook into at least one fish in the 20-inch category. Many of the local fishermen think of those fish as a dime a dozen. The true tailwater trophy hunters are looking for trout at least 10 inches longer with weights over 30 pounds. If I were to brag to them about a 20-incher caught from my local creek, they'd just shake their heads.

When a trout newly arrives in the stream, it doesn't really matter whether he's a newborn or a one-year-old 11-inch stocker. He still has to initially learn how to feed through a process of trial and error. A newborn will learn fairly quickly that midge larvae and whatnot are drifting around and are also quite tasty, and his feeding behavior will develop from there. A stocker, on the other hand, is used to feeding on fish pellets dropped onto the surface of the water, so they're going to have to overcome two disadvantages. First, they'll initially eat anything that hits the water, meaning the survival of a recently stocked trout is in some doubt. In fact, they won't stop feeding in that fashion until they have a fairly close call – being hooked and escaping, for example, or perhaps being caught and released. The second disadvantage is that they're already skillet-sized, so they're less likely to be released than a wild trout of the same age, mostly because the wild fish is going to be much smaller.

Once a trout is large enough to eat smaller fish, they'll give it a try. Wild fish will begin to experiment in this regard at about 7-8 inches in length, but stockers have the advantage of size and will start pursuing baitfish about the same time they realize drifting bugs are edible. And in both cases, this expansion of food options will benefit the trout with added calories, but the aggressive style of feeding will also put them at greater risk of being caught by fishermen using spinners, jigs, streamers, and live minnows. This is perhaps the primary reason that trout generally don't survive long enough to grow to huge sizes. During this time of their lives, they are susceptible to a great diversity of baits and fishing methods. But there is one difference between the trout that is caught and the trout that survives this age range: fear.

It's not the smartest trout that survives this period. After all, even the smartest trout in the river is as dumb as a bag of doorknobs. When a novice fisherman splashes into a fishing spot and hooks into a couple of 12-inch fish, he's not necessarily catching the dumbest fish – he's catching the bravest fish. He's hooked into the fish that did not startle and run off when he kicked over those rocks or waded in too close. The fish that ran – the spooky trout – are the fish that survive. Those that choose to run away live to fight another day. As long as those trout remain "spooky," they'll continue to survive the attempts of most predators and fishermen, and they'll eventually graduate to their next stage of life: piscivorousness.

The term "piscivorous" simply refers to a carnivore that survives on a diet of fish. So a piscivorous fish survives on a diet of minnows and such. As trout grow, they will eventually reach a size where it becomes more and more difficult to maintain their body weight on a diet of bugs alone. At that point, their prior experimentation with eating the occasional minnow or sculpin becomes more of a habit. For rainbow trout, this tends to happen at about 18 inches in length. Brown trout start a bit earlier, usually at 15 inches or so. But in all cases, the actual size depends on the bug population. A river with millions of giant stoneflies or drakes (or tailwaters with hundreds of millions of scuds and sowbugs) can support more and larger fish than a similar river with a more modest population of smaller insects, for example.

This new transitional period during which trout eat more fish and fewer bugs put these fish at a higher risk of being caught. Not only can spin fishermen cast small crankbaits and spinners great distances, allowing them to target nervous fish without having to approach them, the process of feeding on baitfish actually requires these trout to develop a more aggressive attitude, leading to a decrease in fearful behavior. And a brave trout is usually a dead trout.

Luckily for them, this transitional period of experimental aggressive feeding on baitfish is fairly short-lived. Once they reach the next size class, these trout turn into experienced and deliberate (i.e. less aggressive) hunters while almost entirely giving up on grazing on drifting bugs. They'll always eat a drifting bug that comes right to them, of course, but their lifestyle as a calm and confident dominant predator is a radical change, making them a much bigger challenge for the casual angler.

The predator trout gradually develops a new feeding cycle and begins to act very much like a lion. You've seen those nature shows, I'm sure. The pride of lions finds a shady spot to lie around, and they'll spend hours dozing, playing with the cubs, and grooming each other. But, when their bellies start to rumble, they're up and stalking. They leave their resting areas and head toward the hunting grounds, keeping their heads down, moving smoothly and quietly. Any possible prey animal that doesn't notice and gets too close is probably lunch. Once they've secured the kill and fed, they'll retreat to a resting area to doze, play with cubs, and groom each other until their bellies start to rumble once again.

A smaller trout may feed almost constantly, picking at bugs pretty much non-stop. A mature meat-hunting trout, however, begins to eat meals. He fills his belly over a short time and then stops eating to allow for rest and digestion, just like a lion. To translate that type of hunting behavior into trout terminology, we really only need to define the trout versions of "resting areas" and "hunting grounds." Their hunting areas are easy to pick out. Where would a whopper trout find the largest number of minnows, crayfish, sculpins, and fingerlings? The easy answer is anywhere these little guys feel relatively safe and also have access to the drifting bugs that they also prefer to eat. Those areas tend to be deeper water with some sort of structure, and that generally includes pools and channels with rocky bottoms and, preferably, a downed tree or undercut bank with exposed roots.

Big trout do not typically use wooden structure to aid their feeding like a bass would, hiding in the shadows of a downed tree and darting out to grab a bite of food. But they are often drawn to areas with wooden structure because that is often where lunch can be found. Instead of a bass-style ambush, however, they stalk their prey like I imagine a bobcat sneaking up on a rabbit does, extremely slow movements, just a little closer, I'm nothing but a clump of leaves, one more inch, almost there, and then... pounce!

I'd like to be able to brag that I simply figured this stuff out using logic and my mad scientist super villain-sized brain, but I have to admit to observing this behavior during one of my trout stream snorkeling trips. On one excursion, I was able to float almost motionless in a nice-sized pool while a back current held me in place. And while I was observing a variety of average-sized trout doing their normal thing, I gradually became aware of a fairly large shadow slowly moving my way. My first assessment was that it must be a muskrat. Once I realized it was a fish, I was sure it was a sucker, which can commonly reach several pounds on this particular river.

With a very leisurely manner about him, he meandered upstream. He actually seemed fairly aimless. He'd lean to the left a few feet and then hover a moment or two. Then he'd lean to the right a few feet. The smaller fish would give him room, but they wouldn't dart away. And then he made a movement so sudden that I jumped from the shock. He darted forward no more than a foot and jerked his head a few inches to one side with a snap of his jaws. All the little fish freaked out and began an amazing display of what looked like choreographed water ballet, with clouds of the little guys swarming this way and that. I couldn't tell if he'd actually caught anything, but then, as if he wanted to show off, he spit out a small sunfish that did nothing more than twitch a few times, and then he approached a second time and gently took it in.

In case you were wondering, he turned out to be a brown trout that looked to be about 22 inches long. I watched him for another half hour or so and he repeated this impressive performance twice more. He'd drift backward in the current, linger a few minutes, and then slowly move back into the hunting grounds with that deliberate meandering advance. After taking his third meal, he drifted downstream once again and did not return. I waited for quite a while before my impatience got the best of me, so I started slowly moving along with the current hoping to get another glimpse.

I eventually found him. He had drifted downstream a hundred yards or so. The pool had turned into a channel and, as the channel began to flatten out, the bottom gradually turned from rock to sand to silt. And there he was, lying in the silt, right out in the open. I had probably walked right by him earlier in the day, but by sitting completely still, he looked like nothing more than a clump of algae or a piece of wood.

I moved toward him, expecting him to dart away in fright, but he didn't respond to my approach until I was almost close enough to touch him. When I reached out, he simply moved a bit, staying just out of reach. He had reached the age where he was no longer afraid. He had grown to such a size that he apparently felt unthreatened. Now, this was before river otters had been reintroduced to Missouri, so he was probably right in feeling he was the dominant predator in the river.

This lack of fear said to me that this fish should be easy to catch. I should be able to wade over to him and drift a fly right to his snout without spooking him away. But on future trips to this river, I was never able to catch him when I found him resting. Dozens, maybe hundreds, of casts that looked perfect to my eyes resulted in nothing resembling interest. I even managed to hit him in the face from time to time. The only answer I could come up with was that he must be full.

So, while this fearless type of behavior makes these whopper trout susceptible to fishermen throwing baits that imitate small fish, the fact that they have fairly well-defined meal times and rest times takes them out of the danger zone for the largest part of their day. But there is one exception.

These trout can be annoyed into hitting your fly. You can tie on a big bunny leach, for example, and twitch it in his face from an upstream position. Sooner or later he will snap at it. The downside is that most of those snaps are not attempts at eating your fly. They are instead attempts at biting your fly's tale to give it the message that he should "get the hell away from me." A better way to catch these whoppers is to work the stretch from the hunting grounds to the resting area with big slow-moving streamers or big grasshoppers in the summertime, and hope you timed it right. When that lunker's tummy starts rumbling, he'll start moving upstream toward the hunting grounds and he'll take anything that's easy to grab. Since he's so large, he'll also have a preference for a bite of food with a lot of calories. So, any big obvious easy-to-grab offering you can put in front of him will give you a shot at a really big fish. But plan on covering a lot of water.

Now, there is one more age class to discuss here. The legitimate trophy-sized fish that we've just covered changed their feeding behavior to become a meat-hunting predator because that is the only way for them to maintain their body weight. If they get good at it, they'll continue to grow and reach another size milestone. There will come a time when they are so big that they are less able to hunt effectively enough to maintain their new weight, meaning they have to add another feeding style: scavenging.

Every river is full of dead things. If you spend enough time looking, you'll find plenty of dead fish, turtles, and even the nasty bloated bodies of drowned raccoons and deer and whatnot. In some settings, the biggest fish in the river will hang out around areas where fishermen clean their catch, eating the discarded entrails of their cousins. Not a pretty thought or sight, but very common. In other words, some of the biggest of the big trout out there will get the lion's share of their calories eating meat that doesn't run away. They have a fantastic sense of smell if you'll remember. And picking up a bit of meat burns almost no calories at all, so it's 100% gain. This is one reason why there are so many stories about ridiculously enormous trout being caught on natural baits like salmon eggs, marshmallows, and cheese. Those who live near salmon waters know all about using flesh flies to catch big trout or dolly varden char following the spawn. And those of you who fish tailwaters are likely very attuned to hearing the magic words "shad kill." These scavenging trout are on the always on the make looking for easy calories and often it's some lucky fisherman who happens to drop a lump of dough bait in front of him at just the right time that gets the fish of a lifetime.

But, again, shouldn't this make giant trout easier to catch? Well, it's all relative. No matter how big a trout gets, he'll still maintain that hunting-resting-hunting cycle – much more resting than hunting. And if he's feeding five times a day, there's a good chance that two or three of those hunting expeditions are taking place at night. The trout that choose to hunt at night tend to live longer because most fishermen choose to fish in the daylight. And with the trout's superhero sonar ability, they are indeed very effective hunters even on the darkest of nights.

So, if you find a location that some trophy trout call home and you use a great big slow-moving bait, and you happen to put that bait in front of a trout that is leaving his resting place to head to the hunting grounds, he will probably take it. Then all you have to do is set the hook, delicately fight the fish of a lifetime for fifteen minutes without panicking, breaking your line or otherwise losing him to a rootwad, and then finally getting him into your undersized net. And for your best shot, you may be doing all that at night. Simple!

CHAPTER NINE

Where The Heck Are All The Stinking Fish?

As a young trout fisherman, one of the early "truisms" I picked up from the creek's veterans was that when the fishing was good, it was because it was just stocked.

Fish story: I fished all day and I didn't even see a trout! There just aren't enough fish in this river to make it worth the trip. It's been fished out.

I certainly can relate to the frustration of fishing in a stream that doesn't seem to have any fish in it. But I can tell you with near certainty: the creek has not been fished out. There are survivors. In fact, there are more survivors than you think.

By now, you hopefully have a decent understanding of how a fish's baseline level of nervousness helps him to avoid fishermen and other predators, and how each fish defines his own comfort zone. Elementary! Those hatchery fish that survive the first several days of heavy fishing pressure have simply done just that. They've changed their behavior as a simple reaction to what's been going on around them. They've probably experienced a hook in the mouth, making them nervous about feeding. And that's probably led to their super-quick taste test bites and sniff-refusals that drive us all so crazy.

I don't remember what originally put the thought in my head, but years ago I developed a curiosity regarding the survival rate of recently stocked fish. So, I embarked on an effort to take visual trout population surveys on a stocked trout stream not far from where I lived at the time. I have fishing friends that have grown tired of hearing about me snorkeling with trout, but if you've never done it, you should give it a try. It's an experience you'll immediately want to repeat.

Now granted, this survey was very unscientific. I put on the goggles, got in the water and counted the trout that I could see in one specific easy-access fishing spot that received a lot of pressure from catch-and-keep fishermen. Since trout don't necessarily hold still for you, there were certainly fish that got counted twice and there were definitely fish I didn't count at all. And there's also no way to account for the fish that left the fishing spot or new arrivals that migrated in. In other words, since I didn't have the ability to tag fish with radio transmitters, I knew I'd have to overcome the inaccuracies by repeating the process and averaging the results.

I made a few wasted trips because you can't exactly go snorkeling with a dozen people throwing hooks at you, but I found it empty enough times that summer to make the project doable. Twice I found the spot with only a single fisherman, but when I told them I wanted to swim through to count the trout, they pulled up their lines to watch me do my thing. Here's what I discovered:

The biggest number of trout I counted in that spot was around 80. That day no one was fishing at all, so I'm guessing I happened to arrive shortly after the stocking truck left and before word had leaked out. About two weeks later, I counted 20 trout in that spot. That's easy math – 75% of the stocked trout were gone. That could mean they all went home for dinner, but some of those missing fish likely just decided to leave the area. Regardless, there were still 20 trout in a spot that many assumed was empty.

That 75/25 ratio seemed to hold fairly accurate throughout that summer, assuming some of my assumptions were accurate (a dangerous double-assumption, by anyone's account). By the time the fishermen had given up and stopped coming to the creek (about two weeks after stocking), 70-80% of the trout were gone. So, while those fishermen were likely of the mindset that the creek had been "fished out," there was still a good number of trout present that needed to eat and were probably feeding on drifting bugs or the occasional bait fish that got too close.

Other than pure luck, there was only one real difference between the survivors and the fish that were taken home for dinner, and that was simply that the survivors had learned how to live wild. They had learned how to sniff food before they ate it, how to taste things quickly, and how to use the current to allow real food to come to them while they barely worked at all. And, therefore, those remaining trout were mostly safe from the crowd of fishermen that arrived every few weeks with their spinners, wooly buggers, and salmon eggs.

"Mostly safe" does not mean completely safe, however. Some very wily trout fishermen also fished this location – myself included – and we caught fish, simply by looking beyond the 75% of easily catchable trout. That certainly doesn't mean we ignored those recently stocked fish, though.

Whenever I'm fishing a put-and-take trout fishery, I always start off trying to catch the "stupidest" trout first. At a heavily stocked river, that generally just means throwing something out there that is visible and looks edible, so I'll often start drifting brightly colored glo-bugs and wooly worms or stripping a big meaty streamer. If that doesn't work right off, I might switch to a brown-colored glo-bug that mimics the size, shape, and color of hatchery pellets – a low-brow form of matching the hatch. If I'm still not catching fish, then it's a fairly safe bet that the recently stocked hatchery fish are either gone or nervous enough that it's time to get serious. That typically means I'll switch to flies that more closely match what the trout are feeding on naturally, but it certainly also refers to technique.

You've heard most of this already, so I'll try not to bore you. But in general, you're now looking for trout living wild. You'll need to make longer casts. You'll need to achieve that natural drift. Additionally, you'll need to avoid the little mistakes that make a trout nervous – startling sounds, for example. Perhaps the best advice I can give you, though, is to wander away from those heavily fished areas.

A nervous fish that has recently witnessed 75% of his buddies freak out and then disappear is, at the very least, going to hunker down and get tough – especially if he felt a hook himself. A good percentage of those fish, though, will eventually leave the area. And sooner or later, they'll find a new home where they begin to feel more comfortable in their surroundings. That means they're less nervous, which means they're easier to catch... kinda.

But before we begin to wander into the wilderness, why not give those pressured fish a try? While fish stocked yesterday will probably stay schooled up in the area where they were dumped, two-week survivors will not. In relatively short order, they'll identify the primo spots where they feel somewhat safe, where a sheltered area is nearby to make escape easy, and where food is drifting by. Your task is to identify those spots, but you might as well start next to the parking lot and gradually progress into the wild.

Of course, you have some choices to make. You need to select a fly – we've already covered that to a certain degree. You also need to choose where you're going to place your fly. But for nervous trout, the one thing that will make or break your day is your ability to see (or intuit) the take and set the hook with a lightning-quick reaction. There's no description better than what I've already provided that will help you there. Practice makes perfect. There you have it.

So, let's focus on the missing piece of the puzzle: where should you place your fly. We'll start with the big picture and gradually narrow it down.

Most trout streams will transition between the following types of habitat: (1) Riffle; (2) Pool; (3) Channel; (4) Silty Run; (5) Tailout. Rivers with a steeper gradient might skip a step or two. For example, you might find a stretch of river that looks more like riffle-pool-riffle-pool. In those circumstances, the riffle in question might even look more like rapids or even a waterfall. In those cases, the types of habitat will eventually balance out as the gradient becomes less severe, likely with some impressively long channels and silty runs. Not really important, though. It's more important to understand how these habitats transition, and how trout use them to their advantage.

We'll start with "riffles," which is simply where a river's gradient becomes steeper, forcing the flow to narrow and pick up speed. The faster water cleans away much of the silt and sand, leaving behind clean gravel and rocks. Riffles with white caps do a great job of adding dissolved oxygen to the water. It bears noting that rivers with a steeper gradient may have plunges or even falls instead of riffles, by the way, but we'll keep this simple.

Riffles

The vast majority of the bugs that the trout in your stream will be feeding on day in and day out can be found by taking a simple insect sampling in a decent set of riffles, making this habitat extremely valuable to fishermen as a great place to begin figuring out the river.

Trout will hang out in the riffles at times, but they'll generally only do so when it makes sense. Since mature trout are not usually social creatures, they may move into the riffles as a result of crowding elsewhere. And since they can also behave very competitively with each other, you may find them working the riffles looking to beat their neighbor to the next drifting bug. This latter example may also occur during notable hatches. Riffles also have a calming effect, since the broken water disperses the suddenly moving overhead shadows that normally make fish nervous. This light dispersal also makes it pretty tough to see the fish, which is a nice side-benefit for Mr. Trout.

Pool

When the riffles begin to calm down, they generally dump into a pool. Pools are almost always filled with bait fish, and there's usually a solid insect population as well. Many pools will also offer the added benefit of structure – downed trees, boulders, undercut banks – providing places for fish to hide or run to when spooked. Pools are often primary hunting grounds for those fully mature trout that can't really survive on a diet consisting solely of drifting insects. For this reason, fishing a pool with streamers is often a good option for a chance at a whopper.

After the riffles plunge into a pool, digging out a nice deep hole, the current rapidly slows down. The slower current lengthens the downstream end of the pool into a channel. As the current slows, the smaller rocks and sand that were washed out of the riffles and pool will be deposited here, meaning the aquatic insect population may be a bit smaller in this area. Many of the bugs will rely on rocks that they can climb under, but when you start filling in those voids with smaller rocks and sand, there are fewer hiding places.

Little Riffles = Little Pools

Channels are often filled with various obstructions like "lay-down" trees (as my crew calls them) or exposed boulders, and they should definitely be looked at very closely by fishermen.

Not only will you find trout utilizing the obstructions for rest and feeding, mature trout will also move through channels feeding along their way to the "hunting ground" pool upstream.

Channel

If the gradient of the river is somewhat gradual, the current in the channel will continue to slow and the river will continue to deposit smaller and smaller bits of aggregate, the smallest of which is silt. The point at which a channel becomes almost entirely sandy and silty is typically called a "silty run" or simply a "run." To be blunt, it's some ugly water.

Most wading trout fishermen will stomp right on past any portion of the stream that looks like this, and who would blame them? There are very few bugs, usually not much structure to draw baitfish, and, at the risk of beating a dead horse, it's UGLY. But, if you like the idea of hooking into a 2-foot long trout, I would encourage you to at least slow down and take a look. Don't forget that there are some mature trout in that stream big enough that they can't maintain their body weight by eating drifting bugs alone. Those trout typically become hunters – the lions of the river, if you'll recall. Lions need a resting area, and this is it.

Silty Run

Eventually, the river will begin to narrow a bit and pick up speed, and the silt will begin to give way to small rocks and gravel. If you keep looking downstream, you'll see the next set of riffles. But, just before the water switches from slick to choppy, you'll find the "tailout." It's called a tailout because the slick water generally forms a triangular tail (or two or three) as it transitions into the next set of riffles.

Tailouts are important for one primary reason: they are an obstruction for trout moving downstream. Think about it like this. When a trout is migrating upstream, he's looking where he's going.

Tailout

When he reaches a pool, there is plenty of habitat, plenty of food, deep water to help him feel safe – lots of reasons to stop. But if he is legitimately migrating, he'll eventually push out of the pool and through the riffles on his way upstream.

Downstream migration is different. When trout migrate downstream, they're not really migrating in the traditional sense. They are instead simply allowing the current to push them downstream ... backward. This is simply because they no longer feel the urge to stay put or lack the stamina to hold their position in the current. In fact, it's really rare to see a trout traveling downstream unless he's been spooked.

Other than being worn out after seasonal migration and spawning, this downstream movement typically happens for two reasons. First, if the water is too cold (i.e. winter time), their metabolism and muscle control is decreased, resulting in lethargy and a lazy downstream drift. Second, when the water is too warm (i.e. summer time), the dissolved oxygen may drop low enough that they don't have the breath to maintain their position. In both cases, drifting backward through a set of riffles is stressful and those downstream drifting trout will often stack up in the tailout areas above the riffles, in an effort to avoid the inevitable. And when you find them there, the sight-fishing can be great fun!

If all of this information is old hat to you, my apologies. In my years as an educator and fishing guide, perhaps the best lesson I learned was that it never pays to assume your student or client already knows something. More than once I've guided clients who were too embarrassed to admit that they didn't know what I was talking about. I'd say something like "be sure to work the near seam behind that lay-down but in front of the eddy," and the client would say "uh... ok," and then not do it. So, I developed the habit of slowing down and describing every little thing. Then, as the day wears on, I'm better able to gauge the client's knowledge base, and eventually, we can start using shorthand. But, since this is a book and we're not able to talk face-to-face, I hope you'll indulge me. With this general river structure knowledge (and how trout use it) behind us, we can narrow our focus. For example, we know there are trout in that pool, but where in the pool are they, and why?

Perhaps the most historically guarded of river fishing guides' secrets is the "seam." A seam is anyplace on a river where two different qualities of water come together, forming a boundary. That boundary may separate cleaner water from dirtier water ("dirty seams"), warmer water from colder water ("temperature seams"), or faster water from slower water ("current seams"), and in all three circumstances, those seams will affect trout behavior.

Dirty Seam

Dirty seams are uncommon compared to other types of seams. Generally, some heavy rain will swell a drainage creek with runoff, turning it milky or muddy. So, if the main channel is still relatively clear, you'll have a dirty seam present where the two currents come together. Trout will line up along that line between clean and dirty, generally on the slower side, which also tends to be the cleaner side. It's difficult for them to feed on this type of seam, but they will use the muddy water as a safety zone, zipping into the murkiness when they get startled. Aside from this interesting little bit of information, you can probably ignore this type of seam as it relates to actually catching fish. By all means, drift a fly along a dirty seam a few times, but keep moving.

A spring branch joining the main river forming a temperature seam

A temperature seam is definitely more interesting to trout fishermen, as well as to the trout. When a spring branch joins a warmer river channel, for example, you have a drop in water temperature that can change a warm-water fishery into a trout stream, often providing miles of productive water. And that change in temperature can form a barrier of sorts, and barriers often concentrate fish. This is also the case when glacial or snow pack run-off rivers or deep-water dam tailwaters enter larger warmer drainages, but we'll say "spring" to keep it simple.

Now, if the spring in question is large enough, migrating trout will often simply head upstream into the spring branch. But if it's not large enough, or if the spring tumbles to the river or pops up at the river's edge, then the trout are faced with a decision: to continue moving upstream past the spring or to stop right there.

Of course, you already know they don't really care about the water temperature – they're cold-blooded. But when they move from the 54-degree water being introduced by the spring into 70-degree river water, the oxygen content drops significantly and their metabolism jumps. In other words, they fairly quickly begin to experience a faster heart rate and perkier muscles, so they accelerate their progress … right smack into a low-oxygen environment. Suddenly, they're out of breath and sag back downstream into the more oxygen-rich water downstream from the spring branch. Viola! A concentration of fish.

And then there's the reverse of the above example: when a warm water river enters a trout stream and warms it up. The issues are the same, by and large, but with a twist. During upstream migration, the trout must choose which path to take. Migrating into the warm-water tributary is easier on the muscles, due to increased heart rate and metabolism, but if the water is too warm, the lower oxygen may stop the progression. Migrating past the tributary will put the trout into colder water, which will be more difficult on the muscles, but easier on the lungs. For this reason, migrating trout will often move into or past the tributary, only to sag back down into the pool that probably exists at the confluence – which often means there's another concentration of fish.

BUT, if a trout is drifting downstream during the heat of the summer, drifting past the tributary will often put a lot of stress on the trout. Suddenly, the water is warmer, the trout is hungrier, and he's having more difficulty breathing. So, when those trout find themselves downstream during the dog days of summer, they'll be having a hard time. BUT, if a trout is drifting downstream during the coldest part of the winter, the "warm-water" tributary may actually be significantly colder than the spring water. So, when he drifts out of the 54-degree spring water, for example, and into that 38-degree run-off water, his heart rate and muscle activity drop like a rock, as does his appetite.

In other words, during the hottest days and the coldest days, and depending on the size of the warm-water tributary, you might want to fish upstream of such a configuration. That's not a statement on which area will have more trout, but the fish that are upstream of the confluence will certainly be more active.

Trout won't necessarily line up along a temperature seam for feeding purposes, but they can if the conditions are right. If the two currents are traveling at notably different speeds, that's good. And if the slower side of the seam also represents the side with the more optimum water temperature and oxygen content, that's even better. That's because of another uncomfortable truth about trout, although by now I'm sure you'll recognize it as a myth if you didn't already.

Fish story: Trout are like Olympic athletes. They can swim at blindingly fast speeds. No matter how fast you retrieve your fly or lure, they can catch it. Crank away!

While it's true that a trout certainly has the ability to catch your fly or lure, regardless of how fast you are retrieving it, the larger truth is trout are lazy. So, if you're keeping score, trout are lazy, stupid, have crappy eyesight, are not actually picky eaters, and trophy trout got that way by being big chickens. I hope that doesn't make you feel bad about yourself.

That said, aren't we all lazy in one way or another? Don't we all focus more on outcomes rather than process in most areas of our lives? Why do you own a dishwasher? Bottom line, it's because you're lazy, just like me. Why should I spend time scrubbing my dishes by hand, when my dishwasher can clean an entire load quickly, fairly quietly, cheaply, and with a quality that is almost always as good as I'm capable of? If trout did dishes, they'd use a dishwasher, too. And nothing proves a trout's laziness more than a "current seam."

While a "dirty seam" refers to the line between murky and clear water and a "temperature seam" to the line between colder and warmer water, a "current seam" simply refers to the line between two different speeds of water flow. And if you can recognize current seams and learn to fish them properly, you'll outfish almost everyone else on the river. For years, this knowledge separated the trout-fishing men from the boys.

A faster vs. slower current seam is a trout's favorite way to cheat nature. By and large, they're using the same skill that allows them to recognize the size, shape, and location of the marble you dropped in the corner of that football field-sized fish tank. By utilizing that unbelievable ability to sense subsurface vibrations, they are also able to recognize subtle changes in current speed and direction. They'll inch this way or that way, and when they find that seam, they'll naturally pick the slower side. Laziness, in this case, is the quality that allows for survival of the "fittest" – a bit contradictory in human terms.

A current seam is invariably caused by friction. As water flows over gravel, for example, the gravel slows the water. The bigger the gravel, the greater the friction, and the slower the water travels. Pile some larger gravel alongside some sand and you'll have greater friction occurring next to lesser friction, and that transition zone between the slower and faster currents is the mystical magical current seam. It's certainly not as one dimensional as that (i.e. faster water cleans sand out of the gravel and deposits the sand where the current is slower), but all other things being equal – which they never are – friction leads to seams. This type of hydrodynamic occurs all over the place – anyplace where the creekbed is even the slightest bit irregular.

Many of these current seams also act as bottle-necks for drifting food. For example, a rock in the stream causes a very slight acceleration of the current as the water passes by the rock. The acceleration occurs because the redirection of the current moves the gravel and sand, making the gradient in that area just a bit steeper. AND, the faster-moving water just downstream from that rock has to come from somewhere, right? So, as strange as it might sound, that "pull" of the faster current is felt upstream of the rock, consolidating the current as the creek water accelerates toward the rock.

A rock creating twin current seams

In other words, the bugs that may be drifting in the current upstream from the rock may be scattered over a wide area – let's say 3-feet wide. I imagine a bug marching band walking side-by-side. But as they approach the rock, they begin to consolidate their ranks. That 3-foot wide drift of bugs will grow narrower until you have a fairly tight and crowded cafeteria line of food heading right toward and then past the rock. The marching band's formation gradually switches to single file. The bigger the rock and the faster the current, the more dramatic the effect.

The next time you see a spot like this, stop for a moment and study the water immediately UPSTREAM of the rock. Often, you'll find the most dominant fish right in front. Not only is there a current rebound helping him to hold his position – water bouncing off the rock and pushing him forward – but he's also at the head of the cafeteria line, which plays right into that natural competitiveness that dominant fish feel toward their weaker brethren.

A little more complicated

Obviously, obstructions can be more complicated than this. A series of boulders can cause the current to swirl this way and that. A tangle of roots draws water around, over, under, and through itself in a complicated tangle of seams and bottlenecks. A field of watercress slows and redirects the water as well. And when you combine various different barriers, trying to make sense of what you're looking at – trying to read the seams – can be a real challenge. But it's not just obstructions that cause seams. Sometimes they're present for no apparent reason at all.

Take a look at the next graphic of a straight stream bed without obstructions. You'll notice the ridges along either side of where the faster flow has dug the main channel deeper than the rest of the creek. In a gently flowing stream, there may be no obvious visible indication of this variance of current speed, but you can make the assumption that those variations will be there. And the current seams in this situation will roughly mirror those channel boundary ridges, with the slower current, or perhaps even a slight back-current, existing outside of the seams, and the faster current existing inside the seams.

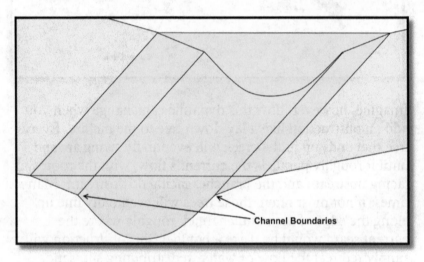

Channel Boundaries

If a trout decides to work one of these seams, you'll tend to find him just barely on the slower side of the seam with his primary attention directed toward the faster side – the side where bugs will drift by more quickly, which typically also happens to be the side with deeper safer water, allowing him to zip into the depths in a moment of panic. Now, while this type of seam will certainly cater to the lazy nature of a trout, it does not form a bug bottleneck. In other words, this type of seam will not necessarily attract actively feeding fish with empty bellies.

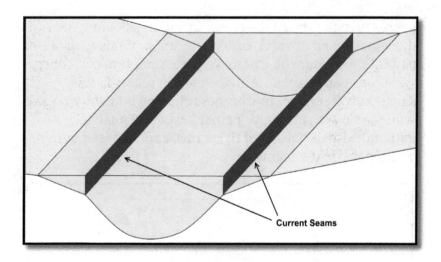

Current Seams

Imagine, however, how this dynamic can change when you add an obstruction like a lay-down tree to the picture. Every tree that ends up in the creek will eventually swing around until it roughly parallels the current's flow, with the root wad facing upstream and the branches facing downstream. Many times, if not most often, those trees will eventually line up along the edge of the main channel, roughly where the current seam would be. Like a boulder, this obstruction will simply redirect the flow of water, redistributing silt, sand, and gravel, which then changes the gradient of the creek bed in those areas, which in turn alters the speed of the water in those areas, helping to concentrate the drift of aquatic insects.

But, because wood is somewhat buoyant in water, the tree will shift and reposition itself as the sand and gravel are moved around. This allows for a much more dramatic change to the creekbed, as the tree will continue to settle into its own hole, allowing the current to dig the hole out even deeper.

Lay-down

In the above photo, the current travels from right to left, hitting the root wad of the tree first. You'll notice that immediately in front of the root wad the water appears darker, indicating a hole dug out by the current bouncing back off the root – much like the bounce-back current that encourages the dominant trout to sit immediately upstream of a boulder – and you'll often find a dominant trout in this location as well.

There's also deeper water along both sides of the log, although it's more noticeable along the far side of the log where the primary current has dug out a nice deep canoe-shaped hole. Since this downed tree is resting close to the nearside channel boundary seam, the faster water is mostly on the opposite side of this log.

While you can look at obstructions in the water and intuit how the current is changing the shape of the streambed, it's always easier to see it firsthand. I've mentioned how much fun it is to snorkel among the fishies, but there's an easier way to study current dynamics. Since every river floods, it should be fairly easy to find examples of obstructions on dry ground when the river levels drop back down to normal. When you have those opportunities, take some time to really study what you see.

In this photo, it's easy to pick out the scoured area right in front of the root wad. And if you look closely, you can pick out the keel of the canoe-shaped hole next to the trunk, with smaller sand and gravel on the slower side of the keel, and larger on the faster side. If you were a trout, where would you be sitting?

I'm sure I've said it before, but I'm going to say it again. I really don't want this to be a textbook, and so I'm certainly not going waste your time by giving you an exhaustive list of every type of current seam imaginable. Rote memorization sucks. But, if you can grasp and begin to internalize how the water moves in relation to the various obstructions it will encounter, and if you use that knowledge to learn to cast to lazy and/or feeding trout (preferably lazy AND feeding), your catch rate will jump from "enough hits to keep me interested" to "downright ridiculous." That said, there's really just one more type of current seam configuration that I want to specifically discuss: the meander.

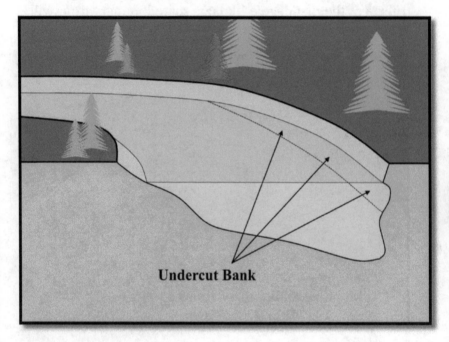

Undercut Bank

There's only one real reason that a river will change direction and head around a bend: a bluff, some igneous bedrock, or another obstruction is standing in the way of the river's flow. That change in direction concentrates the current into the outside of the bend, and that one single quality is usually enough to develop interesting character with a series of parallel current seams, often along with an undercut bank.

Obviously, trout will utilize an undercut bank for a variety of reasons. First, since there are no moving shadows overhead to freak them out, they'll discover an increased calmness when they take shelter under the bank. Second, the friction of the water against the bank will produce a bit of a back current, so the closer to the bank they hang, the lower their energy output. And last, but certainly not least, drifting food will be concentrated along an undercut bank. That's a trifecta of the first degree – a lazy, scared, hungry trout will feel right at home.

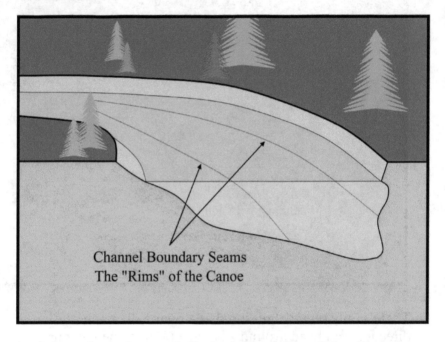

Channel Boundary Seams
The "Rims" of the Canoe

And since the real estate is limited there, those fish will tend to be among the more dominant fish in that section of the river. I'm not being subtle here. Look for the cuts!

A meander's main channel will boast a very well-defined pair of channel boundary seams, just like a straight section of river, but with a twist – literally. Essentially, you'll be looking at a canoe-shaped hole, but the canoe in question will be tipped to one side and bent like a banana. Even so, the trout will work both current seams exactly as you've already learned – holding on the slower side, but looking toward the faster side of the seam for drifting food.

And while you would naturally also try to drift a fly as deep as possible down the middle of the channel as well, the deepest point of the canoe-shaped hole – the "keel" of the canoe – is probably not where you'd expect to find it, since the canoe is tipped to one side. This puts the keel closer to the outside of the meander than you might expect.

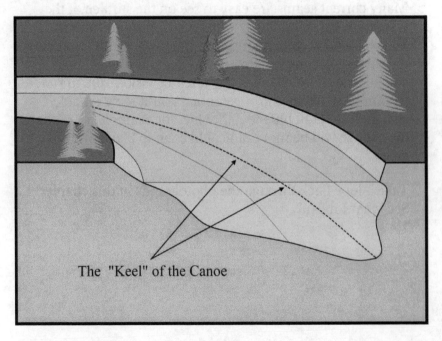

The "Keel" of the Canoe

Just in case it hasn't occurred to you yet, the reason I refer to these types of pools and channels as "canoe-shaped" is not only because there tends to be a "keel," but also because there tends to be a starting point and an ending point, just like the bow and stern of a canoe. And you'll want to keep in mind, as you approach any canoe-shaped hole, you'll find trout immediately in front of the upstream point and immediately behind the downstream point.

If a bluff is the cause of the meander, then you may also find a number of boulders that have fallen into the riverbed at some point in history. Add the fact that a meander will try to collect lay-down trees and debris drifting downstream with each flood, and you may have found some extremely interesting habitat that could hold a ridiculous quantity of fish. All you have to do is decide how you're going to attack it!

Many current seams are easy to see on the surface of the water, but here's one final secret for identifying current seams: look for color changes on the surface and also below the surface. Seams will change the bottom of the creek, of course, and those changes will often be visible due to sudden variations in depth and vegetation. You'll see a notable change from light blue to dark blue, for example, or perhaps the change will be more radical like tan to black or brown to green.

Take a look back through the photographs in this chapter. See what I mean?

CHAPTER TEN

If They're Not Smart, They Must Be Magic!

I'm sure you've seen the nature shows on cable that showcase the miraculous migration behaviors of salmon and their cousins. As one of those addicted to Alaska's salmon runs, I'll be first to admit that it's an amazing thing to witness. But what frustrates me to no end is how these incredible actions are attributed simply to "instincts." After much self-analysis, I've determined that my frustration stems from my tendency toward logic, while the notion of instincts sometimes flies in face of logic. In fact, when I hear someone give credit primarily to instincts, my first thought is that person is indulging in magical thinking.

When a whitetail deer is spooked and runs from your approach, why do they flag their tail in the air? Is it purposeful communication, a concerted effort to alert the other nearby deer to the danger as I've heard some deer behaviorists assert? Possibly. My guess is that a deer simply puckers his butt when tense (like we all do), and that tail jumps up as a result. If the other deer see that white flag and run, it's likely because one deer's tension simply triggers everyone else's butt to pucker as well.

When I discovered trout outside of their traditional normal range all those years ago (Chapter 2), my first impulse was to assume they would be there year after year. Once it became clear that I couldn't make that assumption, I had to admit that there was something I'd missed regarding trout behavior. As it turns out, I had missed the basic logic behind animal behavior in general.

Fish story: Trout rely on their instincts for migration and spawning, finding habitat and food, and avoiding predators. They miraculously "know" how to

_____.

You'll probably notice that much of what we'll be covering in this chapter seems somewhat familiar. That, of course, is because we've touched on a lot of this before. But, as it turns out, I'm the type of person who upon finding a dead horse cannot stop himself from attempting to beat it into submission.

Everything I've written thus far has hopefully led you to logically embrace my one overriding philosophy regarding animal behavior, that the behaviors themselves make perfect sense. If you can't determine why an animal is acting in a certain fashion, you can dismiss it as instincts, or you can work toward trying to figure it out. It's that desire to figure out the trout that has made me a good fisherman. Yes, I can cast and read the water as well as anyone. Yes, I know how to mend my line to get my nymphs down deep. Yes, I know how to properly swing a wet fly. My technical prowess as a fly fisherman is solid, but if I refuse to accept the logic behind trout behavior, then my results as a fisherman will always be at the mercy of the combination of luck and the mood of the fish. I don't like that option.

Fish story: Trout know to swim upstream looking for the spring or the headwaters, because the water is colder there.

Since we've already covered the topic of intelligence, the trout's cold-blooded nature, and his need for high levels of dissolved oxygen (and since I've already referred to this notion as "silly"), I'm hoping that you already can identify the flaws in this theory without my help. But, just in case...

Trout are not smart enough to make educated decisions regarding finding quality water. If the water is "too warm," keeping in mind they don't care about water temperature (cold-blooded animals), they have no awareness of whether that means they should swim upstream or downstream. If the water quality is not ideal, they may leave the area simply because they're uncomfortable or cannot physically stay there, but whether they improve their situation or make it worse is a bit of a coin-flip. Poor dissolved oxygen may lead them to drift downstream, which may push them into warmer lower-oxygen life-threatening water, or it may cause them to drop below a spring entering the river. If the D.O. is good there, they'll stay until something pushes them back out: crowding, lack of food, pressure from fishermen, or maybe a family of otters moving in. The bottom line is that their movements are reactionary, not calculated.

Another one of those nameless faceless graduate students I love so much did a study on an upper Midwest tailwater. They captured and installed radio telemetry transmitters in a bunch of trout, tracking their upstream and downstream movements. Guess what they discovered? Every time the river's flow increased due to power generation at the dam, the trout moved upstream. The degree of movement varied, with trout moving as little as a few hundred yards to as much as several miles. Downstream movement was also recorded and tended to occur only when the current reached extremely fast speeds, or when generation came to a stop, and the turbidity of the water suddenly dropped.

They also noticed something else interesting. As the current slowed, the upstream movement turned into a pattern of wandering or cruising. This was considered to be feeding behavior, and when a trout is cruising around to feed (i.e. chasing stuff), it's what we call aggressive feeding. When the current speed began to bottom out and remained at a more consistent level, they began to see downstream migration. The downstream movement pattern, however, was on the lazy side – more of a downstream drift than an actual migration.

Here's my dime store analysis. Imagine you're standing in a field enjoying a nice summer day, a gentle breeze, a few fluffy clouds, birds singing... got the image? Oh, and imagine you don't have a cerebral cortex. How would you physically respond to a sudden increase in the wind speed from, let's say, five miles per hour to 25 miles per hour? What if the wind speed kept increasing? How would human instincts dictate your responses? Chances are, your initial response would be to turn toward the wind and lean into it. Am I right? If you decided you didn't like the wind, you'd probably leave the field, but your natural inclination would likely be to walk into the wind. So, now you're walking into the wind toward the edge of the field and suddenly the wind speed jumps to 40 miles per hour. Would that be enough to change your behavior? Probably so. You might lay down flat on the ground, or you might turn around and head for the other edge of the field, traveling with the wind at your back. And if the wind speed jumped to 65 miles per hour? At that point, you'd almost certainly look for anything you could use as shelter — a big tree or rock outcropping you could crouch behind for protection. If you couldn't find one, you'd keep moving downwind until you did.

I don't know if this is how you would personally respond, but it appears this is how trout respond to fluctuations in river current speed. I believe a trout's natural desire is to "lean in" to the current, just like you would lean into a sudden stiff wind. These are river fish, after all, so this basic desire to move against the direction of the river's flow makes sense. As the speed of the current increases, the trout react to the change by moving upstream. And if you've ever fished a migration and wondered why the fish don't seem to be actively feeding, the simplest answer may be that they're too simple-minded to manage migrating and feeding at the same time. So, if the current increases over a period of several hours or even several days, a migrating trout may be almost completely neglecting the need to feed. And once the flow crests and begins to settle back down, the stress on the fish begins to lessen and the amount of his attention focused on dealing with water speed also begins to decrease. At some point during this experience, he'll suddenly realize just how freaking hungry he is. So, what we have are fish that are more crowded together than they were previously (they've migrated upstream into smaller water), they're hungrier after migrating without feeding, and the water is high in dissolved oxygen from all the turbidity and/or rainfall. What are you waiting for? Grab your rod!

This is essentially how river migration works. But there does seem to be one major exception to this pattern of behavior. When the increased river flow turns out to be a full-fledged flood, things begin to change. Every fish has a limit, a maximum current speed that they are capable of managing. I imagine that threshold varies throughout the year, depending on their metabolism and oxygen consumption vs. D.O. availability (as affected by water temperature), energy stores (as affected by body fat and muscle mass), and hormones (as affected by... well, you know). But, variables aside, when the current reaches that threshold, the migrating trout will essentially say "enough is enough" and stop fighting upstream against the current.

In both the spring and the fall, we have periodic rains that cause the river currents to fluctuate. Gentle fluctuations trigger upstream migration, while flood waters can trigger downstream drift. Add to the algorithm the seasonally varying levels of dissolved oxygen and things become a bit more complicated, although the movements continue to make sense.

One of my favorite trout streams, the Meramec River just south of St. James, Missouri, has a low-end discharge rate of around 200 cubic feet per second, and I really enjoy fishing it when it's flowing at around 550 cfs. But over the last couple of decades, the river's flow has elevated northwards of 20,000 cfs almost annually, generally in the spring, and it's recently flowed at more than three times that rate. This level of flooding is very hard on the trout. And after the flooding comes to an end and the river is fishable once again, it is sometimes extremely tough to figure out where the fish ended up. The upstream section of the trout-holding area may be stuffed with fish while the lower reaches are empty, but the reverse may also be true, or you may find fish scattered everywhere. You might find them actively feeding in the riffles, or they might be hunkered down in the deepest holes suffering from shell shock. I'm pretty good at making an educated guess, but it's still a little bit of a crapshoot sometimes.

We usually begin receiving some nice soaking rains sometime in late March or early April, sharply raising the discharge to a thousand cubic feet or more. After a few days, the levels begin falling back to normal and I'll generally find the trout exactly where you might guess – a bit further upstream than they were before the rain. I'll also tend to find them somewhat crowded into the upper end of pools or suspended immediately downstream from downed trees and root wads. And the feeding activity is often fierce.

HOWEVER...

As springtime progresses, the ground becomes saturated, the rains become heavier, and there are fewer dry days between storms. So, the graph of river discharge rates begins to look like a stock investor's dream. The trout respond to the increases in current speed with upstream movement, and to the subsequent slowing current speed with more active feeding – just like they're supposed to. But there is a point at which they stop this predictable behavior. When the water speed crosses the magical threshold (whatever it is), the migration stops in its tracks and the trout seek cover. They'll hunker down in the deepest parts of the pools, behind the largest rocks, on the inside shoal of each meander, and at times even in the riverside forest itself if the river overflows its banks. But at 20,000+ cfs, even those shelters may prove insufficient.

Those trout that were previously migrating upstream may find themselves "washed" back downstream, especially if the dissolved oxygen drops as a result of the flooding. Keep in mind that the temperature of the rain will match the air temperature — 40s and 50s is good news, but 70s is not — but the runoff will match the temperature of the ground. That complicates things for the fish. If your river floods during a time when your daily high is in the 70s, significant runoff will yield warm muddy water hitting your fish in the face, meaning you'll for sure see some downstream drift. If the river floods in late July with triple-digit temperatures, the oxygen level drops due to the sudden warming of the river, and trout can be pushed so far downstream into such a low oxygen environment, many will simply suffocate or starve. NOTE: tailwaters are different, obviously. The D.O. levels are more tied to the parent lake's thermocline, in addition to rainfall, meaning you can have the strange incidence of 45-degree low-oxygen water at the dam. That cold water will re-oxygenate as it flows, though, so you won't normally see serious mortality related to power generation.

Getting back on topic, this type of warm-water flood-related downstream "migration" is a nightmare for the trout. The fish will do their best to hold their position, but many will find themselves backing into the tail end of a pool and into the channel. And once the shelter runs out, they lose their grip like a mountain climber on a slippery slope, tumbling downstream through the riffles until they find themselves in another protected area – assuming they survive the tumble, that is. The greater the flood, the more tumbling you'll see, and the farther downstream the fish tumble, the higher the mortality rate.

Meramec River trout are tough by nature and their challenging environment is a gauntlet that turns them into warriors, but the annual mortality rate is pretty high there. I've caught trout on the Meramec that looked like they'd been folded and stuffed in an envelope, at times with a 90-degree bend in their spine – alive, but obviously battered. Those that don't survive are either beaten to death by the river, exhausted to the point that they can't evade otters or herons, or they find themselves so far downstream that they simply can't survive the low levels of dissolved oxygen found in the warmer water. It's the circle of life.

The challenge for a Meramec River fisherman is figuring out where the trout are after a series of flood events. The further upstream a trout lives, the smaller the water, of course. Did the current speed in that area stay below the threshold? If not, how far downstream will you have to go before you find the trout? How far did they fall in the flood? When the rains return next week will they respond by trying to migrate back upstream, or are they too beat up?

Every trout stream experiences similar current-related fish movement. The Meramec is only special in that it floods so heavily, making the phenomena much more pronounced, and therefore much more unpredictable. But if you've ever planned a trip to a favorite secluded trout stream (one that isn't stocked frequently) and found yourself fishing a favorite section of the river that now appears to be empty, you've likely fallen victim to migration aggravation.

Fish story: Trout swim upstream in preparation for spawning.

Here's another one we've briefly touched on. I'm sure you're getting tired of hearing this, but (again) trout are not smart enough to migrate "in preparation" for spawning. That would indicate that they know spawning season is on its way, and it would also indicate that they've established a rule that says they must be in a specific location in order to spawn. The truth is simpler, as it usually is.

Overall, my thoughts on spawning migration are generally where I get the most grief. Quite frankly, we don't really understand it in a purely clinical way, but there are theories that seem to hold up.

As it is with all species, the trout's reproduction cycle is largely dictated by the female. While it's true that some higher-functioning critters will engage in sexual behavior for fun and on whatever schedule they choose, what we're talking about here is procreation. And even humans, who certainly have at least as much sexual fun as any animal, will plan reproduction according to the woman's monthly cycle. Some women even report that they "feel" more fertile and more interested in sex at just the right time of the month.

Trout are on an annual reproduction cycle, of course. Most trout and char will spawn in the spring or the fall, so it's easy to leap to the conclusion that spawning and migration go hand-in-hand. The springtime rains cause rivers to swell and recede, and there are usually similar rain events each fall, although less pronounced. The river's current increases, the fish migrate. The river crests and begins to fall, and the fish stop migrating and feed. A few days later, another rain happens, and the process begins again.

When spawning season is on the horizon, the egg-stuffed females are feeling pretty uncomfortable. At some point, the males notice them, get excited, and start harassing them. One theory suggests the females start leaking hormones into the water, but I'm not aware of any studies that prove or disprove this notion. At some point, the females have had enough of this whole swimming thing, and bow, chicka, bow wow — it's sexual healing time.

In my home state of Missouri, things are a bit more complicated. The state's hatchery program raises two strains of rainbow trout that are closely related – the Missouri Strain and the Missouri Arlee Strain. These fish were genetically engineered to provide two annual hatchery broods, as one strain is a spring spawner, while the other is a fall spawner. This provides our conservation department a good number of stockable-sized trout almost year 'round.

In those wilder rivers where these hatchery trout are placed, you will often find spawning behavior happening during both the traditional spring and fall seasons. But there is another notable group of rainbow trout that spawn in Missouri's public trout streams.

Trout first came to Missouri via rail cars — fingerlings brought from California and poured from milk cans into clear creeks the rails crossed. Legend has it the railroad magnates liked to impress their power base (politicians, investors, rich friends, etc.) by stopping the train and letting them fish for trout in Ozark spring creeks. Among those original stockings were McCloud Redband trout – a species of trout that generally spawn in late December and early January.

The McCloud Redband as a pure strain is almost history, with only a few populations still out there – one of which is found in Missouri's Crane Creek. The rest have been hybridized with hatchery stock. Even so, McCloud genetics seem to be fairly dominant. In those streams where the wild McCloud hybrids still intermingle with hatchery trout, the male hatchery fish will mate with the wild females in January, rather than according to their scheduled spring spawn timetable or perhaps in addition to their recent fall spawning. It then appears that the new offspring adopt the wintertime spawning habits of their McCloud ancestors. And additionally, in those streams that were historically stocked from Missouri hatcheries but are now left alone and managed solely as wild fisheries, the spring and fall spawning behaviors have almost entirely ceased. Cool, huh?

Aside from being interesting, I tell you that to tell you this: January spawning in Missouri's wild trout creeks does not include a major pre-spawn migration. Why? Because migration is largely a reaction to variations in the speed of the current, and the most prominent seasons for that activity are spring and fall. So, on Missouri's little wild trout creeks, fall migration happens quite a while before the January spawn, and springtime migration actually happens AFTER spawning season is over.

In a more "normal" trout stream where pre-spawn migration is the norm, the rains are the first step leading to upstream movement. All the trout in the river will move against the current, but it's the sexually mature trout that will sometimes travel great distances while the smaller immature trout will be more likely to school together in deeper more sheltered water. As the migration begins to push the adult trout into smaller water, the females' estrous cycle will begin to end. In plain English, the girls are so full of eggs that they (allegedly) start leaking hormones into the water while also developing their brighter red spawning colors. The scent of the hormones in the water excites the males, as does the new spawning colors, and those of spawning age quickly split into two main groups. Many of the bulls that have been to this party before will simply shoot upstream and wait for the females to catch up. The younger group will try to nag the females into dropping their eggs by nudging, chasing, and biting at the girls, forcing them to continue moving upstream. But sooner or later, the females have had enough, and after pushing through one last set of riffles, they stop to drop their eggs. As the female drops her eggs into the redd, the male will fertilize them by releasing his milt, and the circle of life continues.

That's pretty much it. Depending on rainfall, water temperature, and flood conditions, the actual spawning action may take place in different sections of the river from year to year, but the general process is the same. The takeaway is that the migration itself is largely coincidental.

Just to be clear, even our January-spawning trout will still engage in some pre-spawn migration. The difference is that their movement is solely motivated by the excited males harassing the females as the magic date night approaches. That generally makes for a short migration, as compared to the more traditional springtime migrations you may already be familiar with. The normal autumn migration will push them upstream, but they're just hanging out at that point. By the time the females get close to the end of their cycle, they'll head upstream a bit more, dig out a red (spawning bed), drop their eggs, and that's that. But for a storybook mega-migration spawning event to take place, you need the rains to come just prior.

Fish story: Somehow, trout instinctively manage to find their way to the exact portion of the stream where they were born.

Well, I have to admit these fish do have some pretty amazing qualities. And while a trout that spends his whole life in a little spring-fed creek doesn't typically have the opportunity to flex those homing-pigeon skills, the physical ability is truly there. Where I part ways with many biologists, though, is in their assessment of what the homingbehaviors are, what they mean, and how they are accomplished. Specifically what we're addressing here is the seriously awe-inspiring migration runs that we've all seen on the nature channels… 257 times. You know the story they sell:

The juvenile salmon of the northwest (for example) drop downstream into the Pacific Ocean where they disappear until adulthood. Then, once they reach sexual maturity, they miraculously return to the exact river of their birth to continue the lineage. Amazing? Yes, of course. Miraculous? Perhaps, depending on your definition of the word, but it's also logical.

Something many folks don't know is that migratory fish have magnetite in their nares (a.k.a. nostrils). In other words, it's possible that they have a built-in compass, of sorts. Migratory birds are similarly blessed. Does this mean these fish and birds use their "compass" to navigate? Almost certainly not – navigation would require a cerebral cortex. It may mean, however, that the direction they are pointing at any given time may affect their comfort level. In other words, if the river of their birth flows west, a newborn trout may become imprinted to the sensation of facing east (upstream). Facing any other direction may simply not feel quite right. So, given the option of heading this way or that way, that specific fish will tend to choose the direction that feels more physically comfortable. Obviously, other external forces exert greater pressure on them, though. Otherwise, every fish in the world would only swim in its favorite direction. The ability to sense magnetic fields is likely just a tie-breaker when faced with more than one potential decision.

To further complicate matters, there are certain river systems that are home to more than one strain of trout – and sometimes these different strains are not hybridized, although they are fully compatible and should be able to cross breed. So what gives? Closely related fish are not typically racial purists, so how are they managing to avoid changing the gene pool?

When fisheries biologists studied this behavior in one specific river system, they discovered that these divergent species each spawned in different tributaries of the river system in question. Why? As usual, no one knows for sure. But, it's interesting to note that the different tributary systems contain different types of substrate and different ratios of certain flora. In other words, the water itself may actually taste or smell slightly different. And since we've already established that trout have an extraordinary sense of smell, it seems a relatively safe bet that when faced with a decision – head up this tributary or continue upstream in the main channel – the more familiar water quality likely leads them into a more comfortable zone. In nature, familiarity never breeds contempt.

I can almost hear your next question. You're wondering about how those ocean-going trout and salmon are able to navigate the big blue, avoid all the sea lions and orcas, and still manage to find their way back to their home river at spawning time. Am I right or am I right?

Well, for certain species, the answer is simple. When they hit the ocean, they don't actually wander too far off – char and cutthroat, for example. Then, when the river swells, they feel the change in the current and head back into it, "magically" finding their way back to their home river. That's the easy part. The difficult part of the equation is that some species actually head WAY out into the ocean. So far out, in fact, that we really don't know where they go. Those fish are still an enigma, but there are theories.

If there is any trout-related area of thought where I know there's a real possibility I'll have to eat my words someday, this is probably it. The most recent research had to do with Pacific steelhead ocean migration patterns, attempting to track their movements with acoustic tags that could be heard by mobile listening stations. But, unfortunately, out of 100 tagged trout, just one was later located in the open sea. The only solid information they gained was the ability to eliminate a specific migration path that they already suspected didn't exist.

That said, I'm sticking with my assumption that even the long-distance open-water migration behaviors of those steelhead make logical sense. Just like migrating waterfowl react to wind currents, air temperatures and the presence of wetlands and other bodies of water, trout and salmon will react to ocean currents, differing water temperatures, food sources, and a sense of safety. And those behaviors will bring them back to their home waters just in time to head home for spawning.

When you look at the primary north Pacific Ocean currents from a two-dimensional perspective, it appears there's really only two options for a migration path. Since they're in a downstream kind of mood when they leave their home river, they might travel downstream, either heading northwest with the Alaska Current or south and then west with the California Current, depending on where exactly their river enters the sea. Or, since upstream is kind of their default setting, they might do the opposite. BUT...

...there are colder currents and there are warmer currents, which makes things a bit more complicated. It's common knowledge that warm air rises, right? Well, warm water rises, too, displacing the cold water, forcing it to sink. And since the sun is ultimately what warms the ocean, it should make sense that warm currents generally gain their heat when they're closer to the equator and shed their heat as they approach the poles. So, warmer currents tend to flow north, becoming shallower as they go, while colder currents tend to flow south, becoming deeper as they flow. So, when you look at a map of ocean currents, keep in mind that the deep blue sea is actually three dimensional, occasionally with a warmer current heading north directly above a colder current heading south.

By now you're aware that colder water better absorbs dissolved oxygen, but the ocean complicates this issue as well. As the salinity of water increases, the dissolved oxygen drops. AND as you increase the pressure (i.e. the deeper you go), the D.O. also drops. So, just as a river-dwelling trout is looking for that "sweet spot" where the water is warm enough that they are hungry and active, but cold enough that they can breathe, ocean-faring trout and salmon are looking for their own "sweet spot" – warm enough for an active metabolism, cold enough for good oxygen, and not too salty or too deep because the dissolved oxygen drops off in those conditions. And throughout these complexities, they're working the ocean currents just like they would in a river.

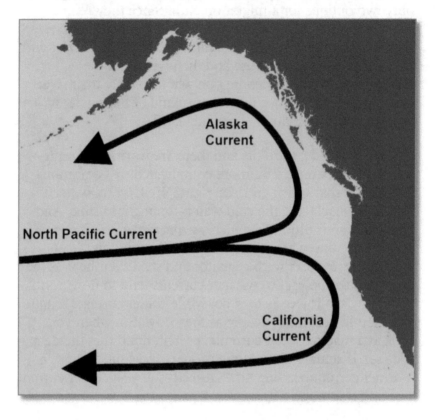

So, it makes sense (to me at least) that those steelhead who disappear for several years are simply following the currents, either upstream or downstream, working to stay in the favorable water conditions that allow them to move, eat and breathe. What happens next is the ultimate mystery. They either start their journey downstream and then reverse course to head back upstream, OR they migrate upstream the whole time and make a complete circuit, swimming "around the block," so to speak. Nobody really knows.

What I do know, however, is that there's no magic involved. Those fish are simply reacting to the circumstances right in front of them. It's no different than when a shadow flashes over the water. They don't think it's a predator. It just startles them, and so they react. After a few years of reactions, they simply find themselves near their home river, sensing the increasing current from their home river via their "sonar receptor" lateral line, and they head home, possibly following their compass and their nose back to the cradle.

CHAPTER ELEVEN

Occasionally, Trout Fishermen Are Stupid, Too

Okay, I must admit the word "stupid" is hyperbole in this case. But if you're like most of us, you'll likely recognize yourself a time or two in this chapter. In general, we're talking about the thoughts, opinions, and behaviors that tend to take away some of the enjoyment in fishing for trout – including our embarrassing habit of looking down our noses at those who don't agree with our personal trout-fishing philosophies.

Fish story: Most "serious" trout fishermen hate fishing in crowded conditions because other fishermen rarely have a basic understanding of manners when it comes to fishing around "serious" fishermen like me.

Sadly, there is confusion about the best way to fish around other people, but it's not really an issue of bad manners. Many serious (whatever that means) trout fishermen actually enjoy fishing in more crowded conditions, or at least they don't mind it so much. In Missouri, we have four public trout parks that are stocked every night — yes, I said every night — in preparation for the hoards of fishermen expected to arrive the next day. This unusual type of fishery collects what can only be deemed as an unusual collection of fishermen, and observing these fishermen led me to the following conclusions.

Trout fishermen can be categorized into three broad groups and all three are present at the trout parks: meat hunters, social butterflies, and lone wolves. The social butterflies tend to enjoy fishing with their buddies, meeting new people, seeing others and being seen. Lone wolves, on the other hand, want to be left alone to stalk and catch a trout in relative solitude on their own terms. While our trout parks tend to draw the meat hunters – those looking to harvest skillet-sized fish for the dinner table – there are plenty of crowded rivers around the world that are strictly regulated to produce trophy-sized fish, thus bringing out fishermen hoping to harvest a giant trout for the wall, although a good number are content with a photograph. It's the same general idea, though. These are waters managed for harvest.

When these three types of fishermen cross paths, there will undoubtedly be conflicts. If you're a lone wolf like I am, it probably irritates you when another fisherman comes splashing over to you to ask what you're using to catch all those fish. By the same token, the social butterfly that just came over to say "hi" is certainly perplexed by that hateful gleam in your eye. Those fishermen who are hoping for a harvest will also tend to be a bit more competitive in nature than others who don't care to keep fish, and when a social butterfly crowds in on them a bit they often respond like they might when a good-looking fella flirts with their date.

Solutions? Easy. First, assume we're all "serious" fishermen. Lone wolves: go fishing someplace else. You know you don't like the crowds. Why are you doing this to yourself? Social butterflies: back off a step or two and ask permission before moving in to fish next to someone. Meat and trophy hunters: chill! It's just fishing, for Pete's sake!

Fish story: Trout fishermen should always engage in catch and release. It's the best way to preserve a trout fishery. Keeping and eating trout is a terrible idea and it's a sure way to destroy a trout population.

Actually, your local wildlife management agency probably has a pretty good grasp on what regulations need to stay in place to maintain healthy fisheries in your state. Their goals likely include providing good numbers of fish, a decent chance at catching larger fish, and providing for a reasonable harvest for the dinner table. In fact, these conservation practices go WAAAAY back.

For years, fisheries biologists have struggled to develop a consistent model for managing a fishery to produce the maximum quantity of meat. In the past, they relied heavily on a fairly complicated formula designed to calculate Maximum Sustainable Yield (MSY). It operates on the understanding that the growth in numbers of wildly reproducing fish occurs parabolically. When the numbers of fish are small, the population growth rate is steep. At some point, the population growth rate begins to slow back down and when the population size is REALLY maxed out, the overall growth rate will stagnate, pushing the population's average growth rate closer to zero.

For the purposes of maximum long-term meat production (i.e. to feed the world), you want to harvest enough fish so the population growth rate stays near its maximum. Maintaining harvest rates in that "sweet spot" is easier said than done, though, since keeping an accurate census of fish is maddeningly difficult and because there are so many unknown variables (the numbers of predators or poachers present, for example). The MSY formula is really just elaborate guesswork.

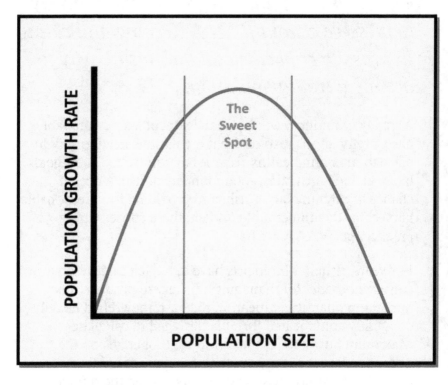

Managing a fishery for food production is not the point of my explaining MSY, though. I really just want you to notice the bottom right corner of the graph where the population growth rate slows to almost zero. That represents saturation, also known as the fishery's carrying capacity. Does that mean that the adult fish stop spawning? Of course not. It likely means that only a small number of newborn fish are surviving to adulthood while sexually mature fish are dying younger, likely from the side-effects of crowding – i.e. starvation or a spike in the population of predators (including fishermen). And while it may seem like a good thing that a river's carrying capacity has been reached, what the sport fisherman will find in that river is not what he's typically looking for.

A fishery's carrying capacity is typically measured in weight per quantity of water (i.e. pounds per surface acre). This measure will vary, of course, depending on the quantities and qualities of the habitat, including forage. I once had a client who owned a farm pond stocked with bluegill, catfish, and bass. He was lamenting that there were no large bass present, but he could catch 12-inchers all day. He hadn't kept a bass in years, but they never seemed to grow any larger. Knowing I had some fisheries knowledge, he asked my advice on what he should do to increase the average size of the bass in his pond. The solution was easy. He needed to start eating some fish. And as soon as the spawn was over the following year, that's exactly what he did.

He began harvesting every largemouth that was smaller than the 12-inch average and filled his freezer with dozens upon dozens of the little buggers. As winter approached, the fishing slowed and the pond eventually froze over. The following spring, the average-sized bass he caught measured closer to 16 or 17 inches.

Again, after spawning had ended, he began harvesting fish, keeping every bass that was smaller than 16 inches long. At the end of the season, he noticed something interesting. He had caught and kept fewer fish, but the volume of fish he put in the freezer looked almost identical to the stockpile he had built up the year before. So, instead of keeping 50 one-pound fish, he had instead kept something like 35 fish that weighed about 1-1/2 pounds each – still roughly 50 pounds of fish.

Among the larger fish he caught and released that season were two bass that were over 20 inches – the largest specimens he'd seen from that pond so far. It also bears noting that he caught a 25-inch largemouth from his farm pond the following season. Now, this whopper bass was certainly of mountable size, but my client chose to release it. A noble decision, to release a trophy fish, but was it a necessary action to maintain the quality of the fishery?

By releasing that fish, my client essentially preserved the possibility that he or someone else could also catch that bass someday, but he didn't really help the bass population. What turned his pond into a trophy-producing body of water in less than three years was the purposeful culling of the smaller fish – DECREASING the competition for resources. Removing the 25-incher would have accomplished the same thing. If that 25-inch eight-pound whale was indeed the largest fish in the pond, removing him from the food chain would have caused one primary effect. Those bass that were one size class smaller would then only be competing with each other rather than with a big bully. And as a result of Goliath's demise, those smaller fish would have all jumped up in size to absorb the missing eight pounds or so of the pond's carrying capacity that had been removed by the fisherman.

You see, true management of a fishery, or any wildlife resource for that matter, often requires a contrarian approach. The default position of most "serious" trout fishermen is that catch and release is the preferred method of protecting the resource. The truth is, RESPONSIBLE and SELECTIVE harvest is the real key. Here in Missouri, even on our most precious trout stream, Crane Creek — the home of those pure strain McCloud Redbands — the Missouri Department of Conservation has determined that fishermen can keep one trout 18 inches or longer. That wouldn't be a dinner table fish, by the way. That fish would be to mount and hang on the wall in your den. Our biologists have simply done the math and decided that this minimal harvest would, at worst, have a neutral effect on the trout population there. Truth is, though, it might actually help it.

Trust me when I tell you that something is eating the trout in your favorite stream. We humans are simply another predator and if we harvested trout like an otter or an osprey would – one meal's worth at a time – the trout population would continue to thrive. Over-harvest, on the other hand, requires additional stocking of hatchery-raised fish to maintain a relatively consistent population. Without it, the natural cycle of population decline and recovery will take place. Even if only a few fish survive the onslaught of over-harvest, the predators (including humans) will leave in search of better hunting grounds and the population will explode until the predators return. Otters, osprey, and herons don't over-harvest, by the way. I know many fishermen want to believe their local stream has too few fish because the otters are cleaning them out. Sorry, but they are a part of nature and they'll find nature's balance. We are outside of nature, which almost always makes us the guilty party.

If the regulations at your local trout stream allow for the legal harvest of fish, don't be afraid to exercise that option. If it turns out the regulation is too lax and leads to a depletion of the resource, they'll adjust the regulations and/or their stocking procedures. If you're the type of fisherman who likes catching BIG fish and also likes to eat a fish from time to time, get out of the mindset that you always release the little guys. Those are actually the fish you want to take home for dinner. And when you eventually catch that trophy of a lifetime that you REALLY want to take to the taxidermist, it's okay. You have my blessing. Really big fish are often near the end of their lifecycle and he's probably going to end up being otter or turtle food soon anyway. But, as in all things, please exercise moderation. If you want a wall full of trophies, there are some darn good replica taxidermists out there.

Fish story: Everyone should use barbless hooks because it increases the odds that trout will survive after being released.

This is another in a long line of touchy subjects, so let's start with what seems to make sense.

When you catch a fish that you plan to release, it makes sense that you want to release the fish as quickly as possible while inflicting the least amount of harm as possible. That means the fish should be out of the water only briefly, if at all. It also means that you should net or handle the fish only if necessary. Obviously, a barbless hook helps to make this possible. BUT…

The greatest risk to the survival of the fish is not damage from the hook, nor is it lack of water, removal of his protective slime by the fisherman's hand or net, or injuries caused by squeezing the fish or dropping the fish on the bank — although those all can cause potentially fatal damage. Arguably, the greatest risk to the fish is lactic acid.

About 35 years ago, there was an exercise show on television called "20 Minute Workout," which generally consisted of three gorgeous women performing a fascinating aerobic dance-style exercise routine while wearing tight clothing that left little to the imagination. I was a teenage boy at the time, which of course meant I was a huge fan – actually, it still brings a smile to my face just thinking about it. That show is the first time I'd ever heard the phrase "go for the burn." That "burn" is referring to lactic acid.

When you work your muscles, your body goes through a metabolic process, first burning glycogen stored in your muscles, then converting blood glucose into glycogen for additional fuel. Once the glucose is gone, it begins to change blood lipids into glucose and then into glycogen, and once the available lipids are gone, it begins to release stored body fat into the bloodstream so it can continue to work toward providing more glycogen for energy. A byproduct of this cycle is the lactic acid that gets you to "the burn."

In days gone by, it was accepted as fact that lactic acid physically damaged the muscles. As you recovered from your workout, your damaged muscles would be rebuilt... better... stronger... faster. That may be true, but there has been a surprising amount of new research over the last few years regarding lactic acid's actual role in metabolism, and some previously radical ideas are now being accepted as new truths. For example, lactic acid is no longer automatically assumed to be toxic. Instead, it's being viewed as possibly the missing link that ties aerobic and anaerobic metabolism together, whereas those two classifications had been considered completely separate and unique from each previously.

It turns out lactic acid is another type of fuel that can be burned by the muscles. In fact, it's a more efficient fuel than glycogen. But there is one ingredient required before the mitochondria (the power plant of the muscle cell) can burn lactic acid as fuel: oxygen!

So, what does that mean exactly? Well, the jury is still out, but it looks like anaerobic ("without oxygen") activity like sprints and weightlifting cause a build-up of lactic acid since without oxygen it cannot be burned for fuel. And because it is acid, it does hurt (feel the burn) and it does cause you to stop moving those muscles once the glycogen runs out. The old school belief was that you needed oxygen to flush out the toxins, but we're beginning to understand that the oxygen simply allows you to burn the "toxin" as fuel.

If the required oxygen doesn't present itself, the acids will continue to do damage and the muscles will begin to shut down. Humans and other mammals are high functioning enough that we actually make the decision to take deeper slower breaths when experiencing these stimuli. Trout, however, are stupid, if you'll recall.

After playing a fish to exhaustion, have you ever noticed how they'll try to turn belly up on you? Their muscles are exhausted and flooded with lactic acid that they cannot burn due to the low blood oxygen caused by the anaerobic fight for freedom. For some reason, one of their biological responses to this condition is to lose control of their swim bladder. And once a fish is upside down, they stop breathing. So, you're looking at a fish with no more glycogen available for quick fuel, very little body fat to draw from, and a whole bunch of lactic acid that it can't burn for fuel when so little blood oxygen is present. Left to their own devices – upside down and barely breathing – those fish will simply give up the ghost.

There are a couple of possible solutions to consider. If you are of the mindset that you'd like to avoid the lactic acid build-up altogether, it makes sense to land the fish as quickly as possible, pop the hook out, and send him on his way. But that may require using a heavier line than you prefer. Since trout don't have good eyesight, that's often a logical trade-off. But if you're fishing little dry flies, the thicker line will hurt your results, and if you're drifting nymphs or emergers, you may not get a natural tumble if you fish too thick. Also, if you land the fish too quickly, you're essentially trying to handle a coiled spring covered with axle grease and the risk of physically injuring the fish increases.

Personally, I prefer to play out the fish so I can land a relatively docile trout. When releasing the fish, I simply take my time. I gently hold the fish in the water facing upstream, perhaps even fanning water into his face with one hand to force oxygen over his gills. At some point, the fish will swim out of my hands under his own power, which is a pretty good signal that he's recovered enough to be out on his own again. Swimming away requires him to burn energy, which would seem to indicate that his blood oxygen has increased enough to enable the burning of the lactic acid for fuel. I'll still keep an eye on him for a minute or two, though. If I see that white belly turn up, I'll net him and hold him up in the current again.

The research suggests that this process may actually be what is best for the trout. In human studies, they've discovered that mitochondria actually GROW when provided a higher than normal level of lactic acid and oxygen, which apparently is what improves endurance in athletes. This could mean playing a fish to exhaustion and then taking the time to revive him properly may actually be a beneficial workout for him, he could be better... stronger... faster... thanks to you. Crazy, huh?

But what about barbless hooks? Well, there are pros and cons, of course. The pros are obvious. The hook comes out easier and faster – out of the fish, out of the net, and out of your hand. The arguments against going barbless are almost always related to the risk of losing the fish, but there are those who also theorize that a barbless hook penetrates more deeply and can cause more damage than a barbed hook, especially when a fish is foul-hooked or hooked near the gills. My own personal opinion is that it's likely a wash.

I've used barbed and barbless hooks over the years and I don't believe I've ever killed a fish with a barb. I also don't believe I've ever lost a fish because my hook was barbless. There have certainly been those times when a barbed hook has penetrated the bony plate of the trout's mouth and in those cases, you'll usually end up doing some notable damage. I'll generally pinch the barb down in those situations so the hook slides out more or less cleanly. And if that situation means the fish is out of the water longer than normal, I'll spend more time on "artificial respiration" to help bring him back. In other words, I don't really have a preference regarding barbs because I don't think it makes much difference one way or the other.

That said, I'm sure you're more interested in proof rather than my anecdotal evidence, so here you are. I was able to track down 19 individual studies that each compared the mortality rate of trout caught on both barbless and barbed hooks. In those studies, fish were caught and placed in large screened baskets in the river and observed for at least three days. All of the studies I reviewed covered at least two groups of fish representing both types of hook and a few of the studies also included a third control group of fish that were shock sampled and not hooked. The study groups included fish caught on bait, lures, and flies using single-point hooks and treble hooks of various sizes. I found no study that reported actively attempting to revive a fish after catching it. Rather, the fishermen would apparently catch the fish, remove the hook, and toss him in the basket. A few of these studies showed enormous benefits to barbless hooks, while a similar number actually showed greater mortality from barbless hooks for some strange reason. Two studies produced abnormally high mortality rates in the 20-25% range, one for barbs and one for barbless, while another two had mortality rates of 0% and 1% for the two different styles of hooks.

After adding up all the sample sizes and calculating the overall results, known as a "meta-study," I found the mortality rate for trout caught on barbless hooks was roughly 5%, while mortality from barbed hooks was around 6% — in other words, NOT a statistically significant difference. Out of curiosity, I removed the studies that had extremely high and extremely low mortality rates and re-calculated, but it didn't really change the overall results. This tells me that simply taking the time to revive your caught fish properly will be the best thing you can do to improve the chances your released fish survives the encounter. And if you play him to exhaustion, you can release him without having to squeeze him, net him, bounce him on a gravel bar, or wrestle with him for 5 minutes while your fishing buddy tries to get a picture. Then, simply remember that a little oxygen will load that fish up with highly efficient muscle energy, as the oxygen makes the lactic acid consumable.

So, my bottom line: if you want to use barbless hooks, go ahead. If you'd rather not, don't worry about it. In either case, keep the fish in the water as much as possible during the whole "pose and photograph" process, and be dedicated to spending as much time as needed reviving the trout that just gave you a thrill. If you'll commit to both suggestions, the mortality rate of your released fish will be extremely low.

Fish story: A "real" fly fisherman only uses

_____.

There are a number of variations to this myth. Those fly fishermen who only use dry flies, for example, often have an air of superiority over those of us who also fish nymphs, wet flies or emergers. And heaven forbid you should use a heavily-weighted articulated streamer, because, after all, you could cast that thing with a spinning rod! Doesn't that mean it's not "real" fly fishing? How about tying on one of those yellow glo-bugs or a foam hopper with rubber legs sticking out all over the place? Heck no! Sacrilege! What about strike indicators and sinkers? Permitted or no? Can you buy imported trout flies at a discount or must you only buy flies tied in the United States? Or even better, you should be tying your own flies! Maybe you should raise your own hackle chickens! Only then will you truly be a "real" fly fisherman!

And, of course, we can continue on down the proverbial ladder to criticize spin fishermen and, of course, bait fishermen are the lowest of the low, right? Among lure fishermen, there are those who cast a spinner and reel it straight back in and there are those enjoy working marabou jigs with finesse around obstructions in deeper water – which is, of course, a more elegant form of lure fishing. There are "sit and wait" bait fishermen who prefer to use commercially made floating dough bait, fishing with their finger on a tight line, their rod in a holder next to their folding chair, and their feet resting on a cooler of cold ones. Meanwhile, there are other bait fishermen who love a single salmon egg on a tiny hook under a bobber, casting upstream and drifting it back toward them, fishing much like a suspension-style nymph fisherman would. But that's cheating, right? He's nymph fishing with bait and a spinning rod! But at least it's better than using corn or marshmallows. Am I right or am I right?

Well, the funny thing is that it doesn't matter how much of a purist you think you are, there is always someone else out there who is purer and more than eager to point out your short-comings. I've been criticized on the river by complete strangers because the arbor of my reel was larger than what they thought I needed. I've also been shamed for using a graphite rod – bamboo is obviously the way to go if you want to be a "real" fly fisherman. I once even knew a man that raised silkworms in his basement to braid his own fly line. Even though it's kind of ridiculous, I have to admit that last one is pretty darn cool.

How about this one? Have you ever posted a picture of a large trout on social media... on a stringer? What kind of response did you receive? Have you recovered yet?

For God's sake people, just catch the freaking fish! Do your own thing and stop worrying about what everyone else is up to! If your neighbor on the river is following the rules and fishing legally, you simply don't have any right to judge.

Dave Whitlock is considered by many to be the grandfather of modern American fly-fishing and with good reason. Aside from his book- and article-writing and successful multi-decade career as a fly-fishing guide and instructor, he's also been repeatedly recognized as one of the sport's premier conservationists. He invented an in-stream trout egg incubator to help reseed trout streams to develop naturally reproducing trout populations and he created dozens upon dozens of trout flies, many of which are now industry standards: Dave's Hopper, the Matuka Sculpin, the Red Fox Squirrel Hair Nymph, and the Near Nuff Crayfish being among the most popular.

Dave first started experimenting with fishing nymphs in the 1950s, but he wasn't able to see the hits. In those days, if you weren't fishing a tight line you either had to see the fish actually move to the fly or you'd watch the fly line and leader for additional visual cues for a take. Some would grease their leader to make the monofilament visible at the point where it submerges below the surface. His inability to see the hits using these methods led him to experiment with fishing brightly colored fly lines. When that didn't prove beneficial enough, he tried coloring the tip of the line with fluorescent paint. That was a little better but still not quite there. Finally, he began attaching some brightly colored yarn onto the leader itself. It turns out that was the real ticket. And while he was continuing to fine-tune his new system, Dave remembers that he "caught all kinds of hell" from his fellow fishermen for using a "bobber." But what Dave had actually done is invent the strike indicator.

So you see, even some of the greatest thinkers of the modern fly-fishing era had to deal with the scorn of "purists." My advice to you is to be as pure as you want to be, but do your best to leave the scorn at home. We're all just trout fishermen, after all! And since trout are stupid, lazy cowards, we can't be all that great, can we?

Fish story: Trout fishing is somehow a more noble pursuit than fishing for other fish like bass, catfish or crappie. Therefore, trout fishermen are nobler. After all, it's a gentleman's sport!

Okay… yeah… that one's true.

EPILOGUE

Now What?

My wife might tell you this book has been, to one degree or another, the bane of my existence. I wrote my first draft ten years before this final version. I edited it myself and was pretty happy with it, except for one thing. There was one assertion I was making in the manuscript that I just couldn't back up scientifically at all. It was strictly my gut talking along with some anecdotal evidence. I struggled with the idea of removing the information altogether, leaving it in along with a strenuous disclaimer to guard against future research that might prove embarrassing, or just digging in to try to adequately prove my theory somehow. So the manuscript sat while I continued fishing, experimenting, and reading in an effort to clarify the issue in question. Eventually, new research was published that seemed to support my thinking, so all was good. BUT...

During those few years of delay, other new research came to light that seemed to dispute another of my ideas. The more time I spent studying the research, the more I came to believe the research itself was flawed. My pride kept pushing me to ignore it or at least to address it and explain why I didn't buy it. More delays while I struggled with my trout theories, all the while trying to remain aware of how cognitive dissonance rears its ugly head when we don't want to let go of a "sacred belief."

As more researchers and writers began addressing this new area, I began to tweak my trout-related belief system accordingly, and FINALLY managed to produce a manuscript I was happy with. But then I came up with one last self-imposed delay. I began worrying about publishing these thoughts only to have them questioned or ridiculed as new researchers began trying to prove or disprove some of these theories. I'm not afraid of criticism, and I have no problem issuing a second edition with corrected information, but I just had this sinking feeling that the day after publication one of those nameless faceless fisheries graduate students that I love so much would release something new that would cause me to chuck a few thousand printed books in the dumpster (an expensive proposition). So I again decided to let things percolate. I re-read the manuscript more times than I can recall and continued to fine-tune its flow, and I kept reading research papers, but nothing has happened to change my mind on these issues. So now after ten years, I'm finally happy and content with what I've written — with one exception. I haven't answered an important question: "what do I want people to do with this information?"

Of course, I'm hoping this sparks your curiosity about why trout do what they do. If there's anything in this book that you simply can't accept, dig and do some research. Prove me wrong. And send me an email to let me know. I promise I'll leave my cognitive dissonance at the door and give you a fair shake. I'll even credit you with helping me figure out the trout when I publish edition #2 in another ten years.

The other thing I'm hoping this information accomplishes is more simplistic. I'm hoping it helps you have more fun fishing for trout. And with that in mind, I'm going to provide you with my personal process for problem-solving a strange trout stream using the information from this book. This will all look familiar to you by now, but hopefully putting it in a step-by-step format will help. Here y'ar:

1. Pre-trip research

Once you've identified where you plan to fish you need to learn all you can about it. I'm not talking about tracking down a list of favorite fly patterns, here. I'm talking about identifying water temperature, river pH, forage, typical river flow fluctuations you can expect, major hatches happening during the time you'll be there, when the fish typically spawn, access points, and so on.

For what it's worth, the more alkaline the river is the more aquatic insects and crustaceans you'll find in the water column. The reason this is important is probably something you've overlooked. If there is an abundance of food drifting directly to the trout's nose, they have no real reason to look to the surface for food, so dry fly fishing is probably not going to be your first choice of tactics — unless there's a hatch going on.

2. Pick your access point

Look at the recent weather patterns. How much rain has the area been receiving over the last month or so? What has the air temperature been like? Check out the USGS river levels website. How much river fluctuations have they been seeing? What can you intuit from this information that will help you identify where the best concentrations of fish might be? Will they be crowded upstream? Will they be in the pools or the riffles? Which access points will put you in the right zone?

3. Streamside research

Once you've arrived at your first river access point it's time to settle into some observation time. How many other fishermen do you see? Crowds of fishermen tend to indicate crowds of fish, but they also indicate pressured fish. That can mean the bites will be lightning quick. Seeing no other fishermen on the river could be a great thing, or it might mean they know something you don't know. Is there a high bank you can get on to look down into the water to observe trout behaviors? Are there some shallow riffles where you can sample the bug population? Is there a nearby fisherman you can ask for advice? Yes, you're allowed to do that. Ultimately, you're trying to decide if you'd like to fish this spot or if you should try the next one.

4. Testing the trout

Once you're ready to hit the water, it's time to determine what kind of feeding behavior the trout are engaging in and what fly you should be using. If you know there's a major hatch going on, you can skip this step. Just fish the hatch.

a)   Are they feeding aggressively? You can test this by wading downstream and casting streamers across the current, mending to allow them time to sink, and stripping them back to you across the swing. Try a number of different retrieval techniques: long aggressive strips, quick short strips, twitching, drifting and swinging without action, etc. Adjust your depth by adding weight or casting a bit more upstream or downstream rather than straight across the current. Try a few different flies, too. Different sizes, different colors. If the trout are feeding aggressively, they'll usually demonstrate a willingness to grab whatever they see, but you can help them notice your fly by fishing dark colors on overcast days, flashier or lighter colors on bright days, and occasionally matching the color and size of a primary forage target. Don't waste a ton of time on this stage, though. If they're chasing food, they'll let you know fairly quickly.

b) If they're not pursuing food, are they feeding opportunistically? This style of feeding simply means they're willing to taste anything that looks like it might be edible, as long as they don't have to chase it. It's at this stage that you try out some silly flies: a Y2K Bug, a Chamois Worm, a Girdle Bug. You get the idea. Just pick something that is easy to spot and looks like it might be tasty. Is the water fairly warm? Remember, warm water means hungry fish. It might pay to pick a big fly. A tandem rig can be beneficial here, using a big silly pattern as your lead fly, and trailing something smaller and more natural-looking behind it. Let the fish tell you what they prefer.

c) If they're not feeding opportunistically, then they're probably feeding naturally. Start choosing flies that represent the natural forage they see every day — if you took that bug sample during step 3, you'll know exactly which flies to pick. Start with larger options like stoneflies or drakes and work your way down in size. You can continue with the tandem fly technique, but the silly flies should have been put away by this point. Lead with larger flies and trail smaller flies behind.

d) If things are still not working, it probably means they're feeding selectively. Do you see any feeding behavior happening? Any chance there's a hatch going on that hasn't broken out into the air yet? Nymphs swimming to the surface? Emergers? Do you see any dimples on the water? Is there something else going on? A scud migration?

5. Reassessing the situation

If you're still not having any luck, it's time for a bit of self-reflection. How's your technique? Are you spooking the fish? Wading in too far? Making too much noise with your casting or mending? Did you pick the wrong access point? Or are they even biting at all? Should you hit the local fly shop for some advice? Something has to change – most likely it's your efforts, your location, or the time of day. And always remember the two biggest things you can do to improve your catch rate are (1) add another sinker, and (2) set the hook twice as often.

6. Getting some help

If you still can't figure it out, hire a quality guide and make sure he explains his process to you in great detail. You'll probably feel silly when you figure out the missing piece of the puzzle, but that's okay. That's why guides exist.

If all else fails, shoot me an email. In the immortal words of Viper: "Maverick, you'll get your RIO when you get to the ship. And if you don't, give me a call. I'll fly with you."

Walt Fulps
walt@MissouriTroutHunter.com

SOURCES

I know I've said it a few times already, but this was never meant to be a textbook. Even so, I know there will be a few assertions I've made here that may raise an eyebrow or two. So, for those of you who are research junkies like I am, here y'ar. This is my scholarly bibliography. I've read plenty of trout fishing books as well, over the years, but this list is where my hardcore knowledge comes from. I can't promise that you'll find book-information in each of these sources, but I can promise that you'll find interesting information to help you on your journey of "figuring out the trout."

A Fishy Sixth Sense: Why you can't sneak up on a fish; Michael Symes; X-Ray Magazine.

Acceleration performance of rainbow trout and green sunfish; P.W. Webb; Journal of Experimental Biology.

An evaluation of a high-quality fishery in Missouri; Larry Gale, Charles Purkett Jr., Dan Dickneite, James Fry; Missouri Department of Conservation.

Anthropomorphic denial of fish pain; Lynn Sneddon, Matthew Leach; Animal Sentience.

Assessment of movements of resident stream brown trout among contiguous sections of stream; J.H. Knouft, J.R. Spotila; Ecology of Freshwater Fish.

Bear Valley Westslope Cutthroat Trout: Migration, Spawning, and Habitat; Caleb Surstadt, Kirsten Stephan; USDA Forest Service, Trout Unlimited, Idaho Department of Fish and Game.

Brainstem lateral line responses to sinusoidal wave stimuli in still and running water; Sophia Krother, Joachim Mogdans, Horst Bleckmann; Institute for Zoology, University of Bonn.

Color Vision in Trout and Salmon; Gary Borger; FineFishing.com.

Contrasting movement and activity of large brown trout and rainbow trout in Silver Creek, Idaho; Michael K. Young, Richard A. Wilkison, J.M. Phelps III, J.S. Griffith; Great Basin Naturalist.

Dead Wood Dynamics in Stream Ecosystems; Robert Naiman, Estelle Balian, Krista Bartz, Robert Bilby, Joshua Latterell; USDA Forest Service General Technical Report.

Designing Trout Flies; Gary Borger.

Directional variant and invariant hearing thresholds in the rainbow trout; Nico A.M. Schellart, Rob J.A. Buwalda; The Company of Biologists.

Dispersal of brook trout in rehabilitated streams in Great Smoky Mountains National Park; S.E. Moore, G.L. Larson, B. Ridley; Journal of the Tennessee Academy of Science.

Do Fish Feel Pain?; James Rose; Reviews of Fisheries Science.

Downstream displacement of post-emergent brown trout: Effects of development stage and water velocity; M. Daufresne, H. Capra, P. Gaudin; Journal of Fish Biology.

Effect of Noxious Stimulation Upon Antipredator Responses and Dominance Status in Rainbow Trout; Paul Ashley, Sian Ringrose, Katie Edwards, Emma Wallington, Catherine McCrohan, and Lynne Sneddon; The Humane Society Institute for Science and Policy, Animal Studies Repository.

Environmental requirements and tolerances of Rainbow trout and Brown trout with special reference to Western Australia: A review; Brett Molony; Department of Fisheries, Government of Western Australia, Fisheries Research Division.

Fish Vision and the Salmonids; Dave Wallbridge; Sexy Loops Magazine.

Genetic Diversity Among Hatchery Stocks and Established Populations of Rainbow Trout in Missouri; Casey Dillman, Jeffrey Koppelman; Transactions of the American Fisheries Society.

Healing Troubled Waters; A Report by Trout Unlimited, Arlington, VA.

Homing movements of displaced stream-dwelling brown trout; J.D. Armstrong, N.A. Herbert; Journal of Fish Biology.

Identification of an Independent Population of Sockeye Salmon in Lake Ozette, Washington; Kenneth Currens, Robert Fuerstenberg, William Graeber, Kit Rawson, Mary Ruckelshaus, Norma Sands, James Scott; NOAA Technical Memorandum.

Independent Populations of Chinook Salmon in Puget Sound; Mary Ruckelshaus, Kenneth Currens, William Graeber, Robert Fuerstenberg, Norma Sands, James Scott; NOAA Technical Memorandum.

Kootenai River Fisheries Investigations: Salmonid Studies; Vaughn Paragamian, Jody Walters, Melo Maiolie, Kirk Handley, Matthew Campbell, Christine Kozfkay, Eric Tretter; Idaho Department of Fish and Game.

Landscapes to Riverscapes: Bridging the Gap Between Research and Conservation of Stream Fishes; Kurt D. Fausch, Christian E. Torgersen, Colden V. Baxter, Hiram W. Li; Journal of Bioscience.

Life history of wild rainbow trout in Missouri; Larry Gale, Charles Purkett, Dan Dickneite, James Fry; Missouri Department of Conservation.

Migration of anadromous brown trout Salmon trutta in a Norwegian river; N. Jonsson, B. Jonsson; Freshwater Biology.

Movements of Fluvial Bonneville Cutthroat Trout in the Thomas Fork of the Bear River, Idaho–Wyoming; Warren T Colyer, Jeffrey Kershner, Robert Hilderbrand; North American Journal of Fisheries Management 25:954-963, 2005.

Natural reproduction of rainbow trout; Spencer Turner; Missouri Department of Conservation.

Nine-spined sticklebacks deploy a hill-climbing social learning strategy; Jeremy Kendal, Luke Rendell, Thomas Pike, Kevin Laland; Behavioral Ecology.

Observations of movements of wild trout in two Michigan stream drainages; D. S. Shetter; Transactions of the American Fisheries Society.

Ocean Ecosystem Indicators of Salmon Marine Survival in the Northern California Current; Bill Peterson, JoAnne Butzerin, Edmundo Casillas, John Ferguson; Northwest Fisheries Science Center, NOAA Fisheries Service.

Oxygen Consumption and Swimming Performance in Hypoxia-Acclimated Rainbow Trout; P.G. Bushnell, J.F. Steffensen, K. Johansen; The Company of Biologists.

Rainbow trout in a regulated river below Glen Canyon Dam, Arizona, following increased minimum flows and reduced discharged variability; T. McKinney, D.W. Speas, R.S. Rogers, W.R. Persons; North American Journal of Fisheries Management.

Repeat homing of brown trout in Lake Encumbene, New South Isles, Australia; R.D.J. Tilzey; Journal of the Fisheries Research Board of Canada.

Review of Fish Behavior Relevant to Fish Guidance Systems; Blake Feist, James Anderson; Fisheries Research Institute.

Salmon Recovery Science Review Panel; Joe Travis, Russell Lande, Marc Mangel, Ransom Myers, Pete Peterson, Mary Power, Dan Simberloff, Beth Sanderson; Southwest Fisheries Science Center, National Marine Fisheries Service.

Seasonal migrations of adult and sub-adult redband trout in a high desert basin of Eastern Oregon, USA; M. Anderson, G. Giannico, S. Jacobs; Ecology of Freshwater Fish.

Spatial Distribution and Species Segregation of Bonneville Cutthroat Trout, Brown Trout, and Brook Trout; R. Lokteff, Joseph Wheaton, B.B. Roper; American Fisheries Society 141st Annual Meeting.

Spawning migration and habitat use of adfluvial brown trout, Salmo trutta, in a strongly seasonal boreal river; Maare Saraniemi, Ari Huusko, Heikki Tahkola; Finnish Game and Fisheries Research Institute.

Status review of chum salmon from Washington, Oregon, and California; Orlay Johnson, Stewart Grant, Robert Kope, Kathleen Neely, William Waknitz, Robin Waples; National Marine Fisheries Service, Northwest Fisheries Science Center, Conservation Biology Division.

Status review of west coast steelhead from Washington, Idaho, Oregon, and California; Peggy Busby, Thomas Wainwright, Gregory Bryant, Lisa Lierheimer, Robin Waples, William Waknitz, Irma Lagomarsino; National Marine Fisheries Services, Northwest Fisheries Science Center, Coastal Zone, and Estuarine Studies Division.

Stream fish occurrence in response to impervious cover, historic land use, and hydrogeomorphic factors; Seth Wenger, James Peterson, Mary Freeman, Byron Freeman, David Homans; Canadian Journal of Fisheries and Aquatic Science.

The Effects of Motorized Watercraft on Aquatic Ecosystems; By Timothy Asplund; Wisconsin Department of Natural Resources, Bureau of Integrated Science Services.

The leaping behavior of salmon and trout at falls and obstructions; T.A. Stuart; Department of Agriculture and Fisheries for Scotland.

The spawning migration of anadromous rainbow trout in the Santa Cruz River, Patagonia (Argentina) through radio tracking; Carla Riva Rossi, Milagros Arguimbau, Miguel Pascual; Asociacion Argentina de Ecologia.

Tracking steelhead migration from the Columbia River through the Pacific Ocean: a pilot study; Michelle Rub, Laurie Weitkamp, David Teel, Lyle Gilbreath, Paul Bentley, Marisa Litz, Andrew Claxton, Lila Charlton, Brian Kelly, Rick Nelson; Northwest Fisheries Science Center.

Training, Speed, and Stamina in Trout; R. Bainbridge; Journal of Experimental Biology.

PHOTOS & GRAPHICS

Other than those listed below, all photographs and graphics are by Walt Fulps

About the Author

Walt Fulps was born in San Diego, California to a military family. He discovered trout when stationed at Fort Leonard Wood, Missouri, during elementary school and began teaching himself to fly fish in 1978. He graduated from Southwest Missouri State University in 1992 with a degree in Therapeutic Recreation and spent most of his early career working in the areas of experiential and adventure therapy.

After returning to the Missouri Ozarks in 2002, he designed and published the website **www.MissouriTroutHunter.com** and almost immediately began developing a following. He's been guiding, teaching, and writing about trout and fly fishing ever since, and he also takes groups of clients to Prince of Wales Island, Alaska every September for the annual coho salmon run.

Walt's been married to his best friend Linda for more than 26 years, and they have one son, Patrick, studying Computer Science at Missouri University of Science and Technology.

In addition to the website, you can connect with Walt in the following ways:

Facebook: www.facebook.com/MoTroutHunter
Twitter: twitter.com/MOTroutHunter
LinkedIn: www.linkedin.com/in/waltfulpsmotrouthunter
Instagram: www.instagram.com/missouritrouthunter
Article Samples: https://waltfulps.contently.com